FOR ORGANS, PIANOS & ELECTRONIC KEYBOARDS

E-Z PLAY TODAY

130

Taylor Hits

MW00851176

ISBN 978-1-4803-2985-0

HAL•LEONARD®
CORPORATION

7777 W. BLUEMOUND RD. P.O. BOX 13819 MILWAUKEE, WI 53213

E-Z Play® Today Music Notation © 1975 by HAL LEONARD CORPORATION
E-Z PLAY and EASY ELECTRONIC KEYBOARD MUSIC are registered trademarks of HAL LEONARD CORPORATION.

Visit Hal Leonard Online at
www.halleonard.com

Back to December

Registration 8
Rhythm: Ballad

Words and Music by
Taylor Swift

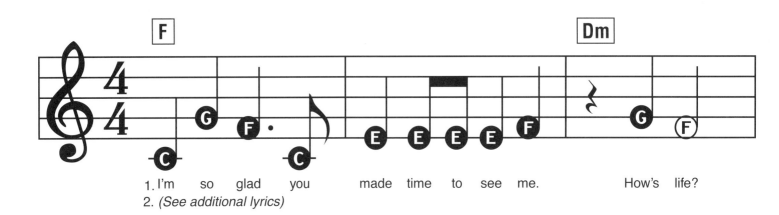

1. I'm so glad you made time to see me. How's life?
2. *(See additional lyrics)*

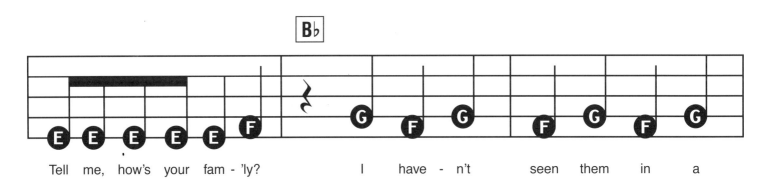

Tell me, how's your fam - 'ly? I have - n't seen them in a

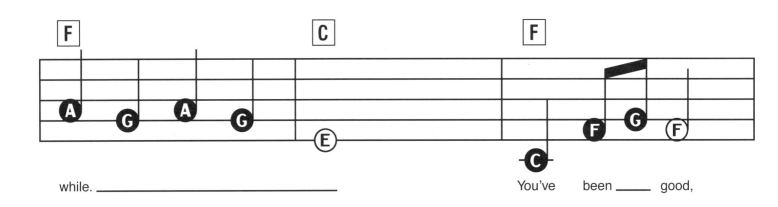

while. _____ You've been ____ good,

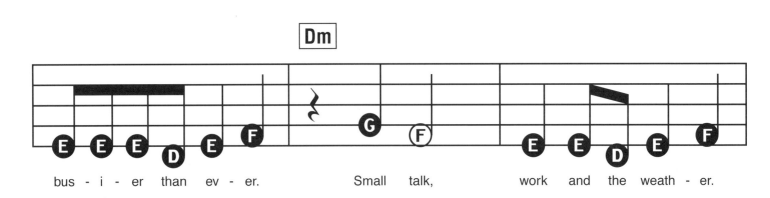

bus - i - er than ev - er. Small talk, work and the weath - er.

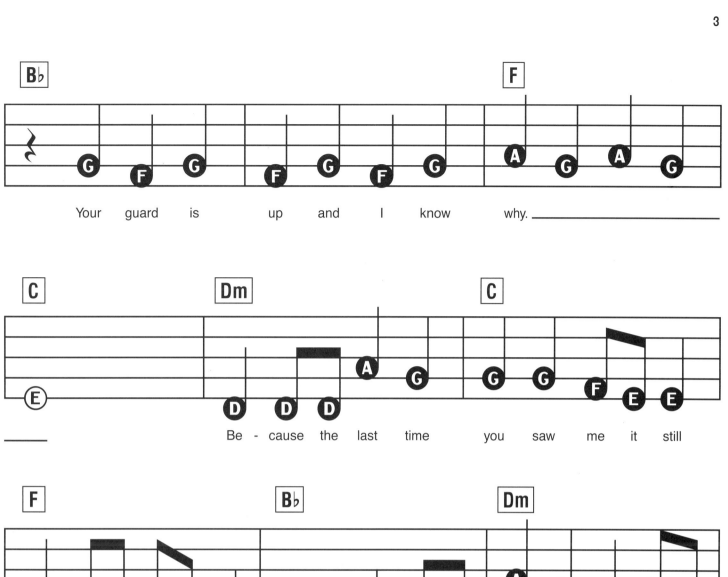

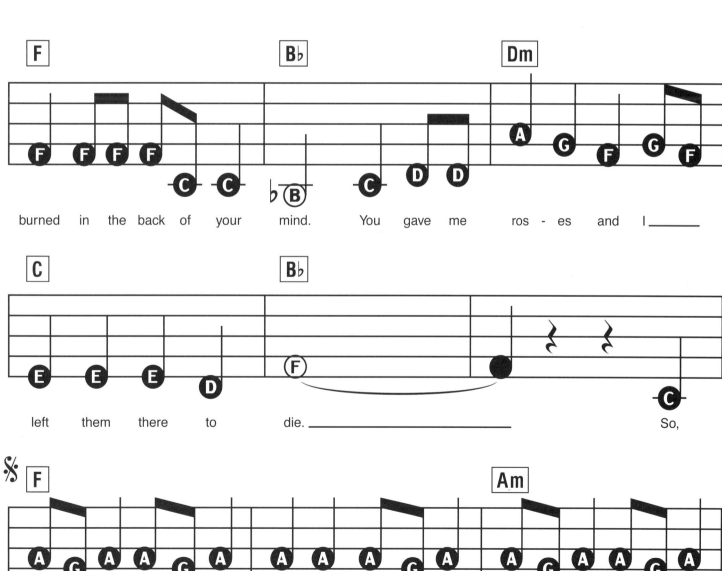

4

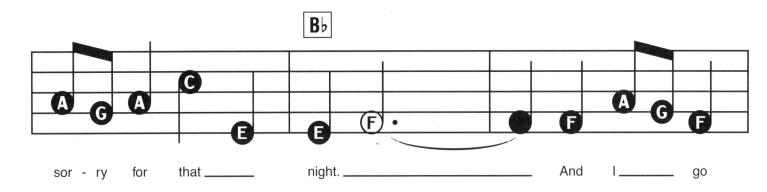

sor - ry for that _____ night. _____ And I _____ go

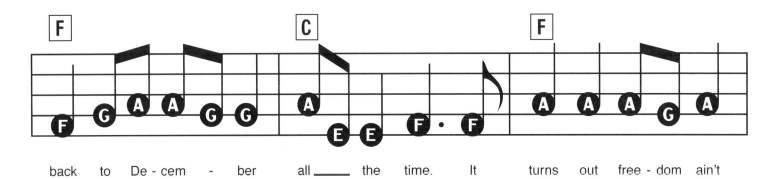

back to De - cem - ber all _____ the time. It turns out free - dom ain't

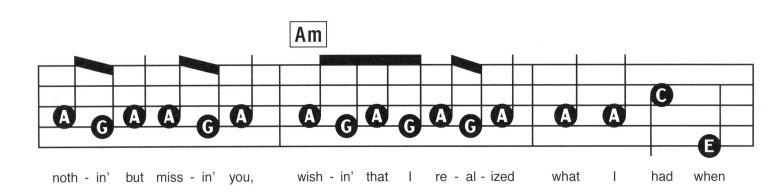

noth - in' but miss - in' you, wish - in' that I re - al - ized what I had when

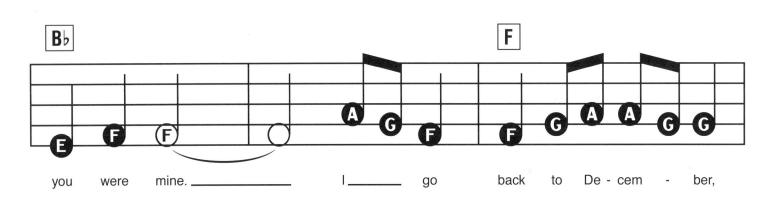

you were mine. _____ I _____ go back to De - cem - ber,

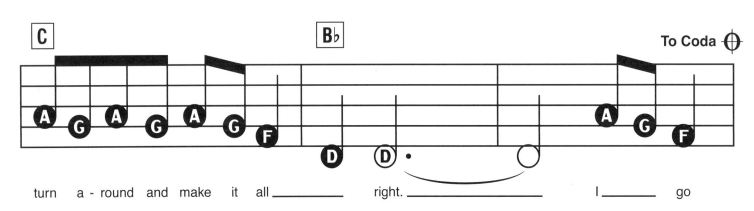

turn a - round and make it all _____ right. _____ I _____ go

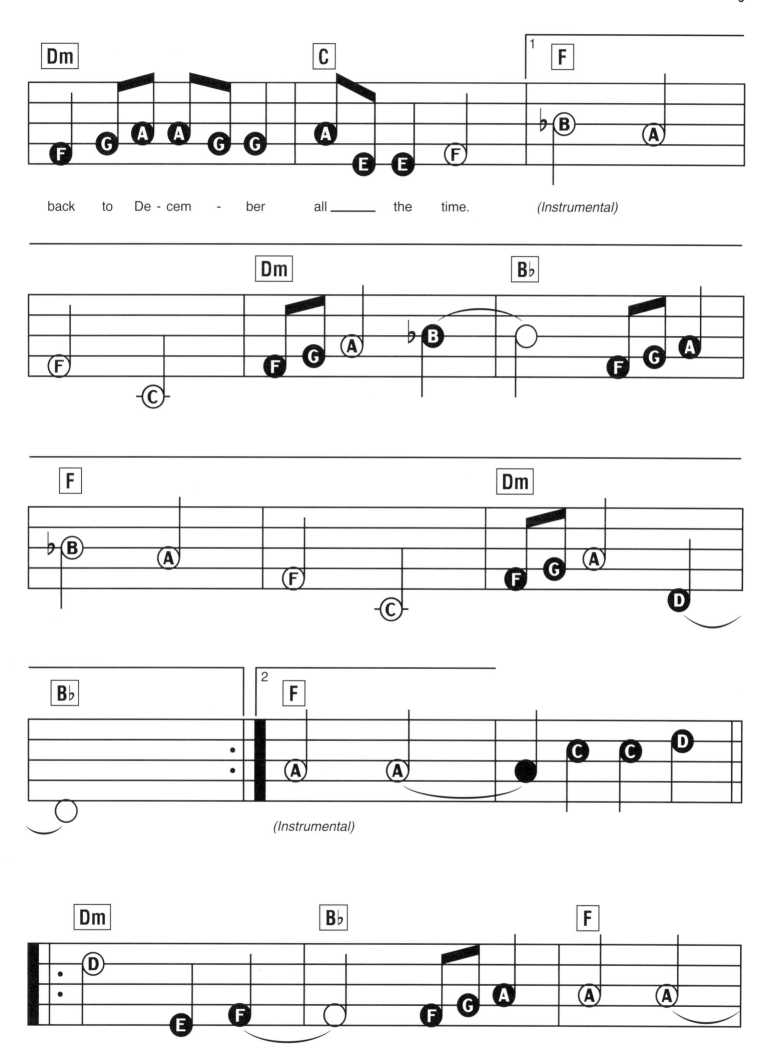

back   to   De - cem - ber   all ____ the   time.   *(Instrumental)*

(Instrumental)

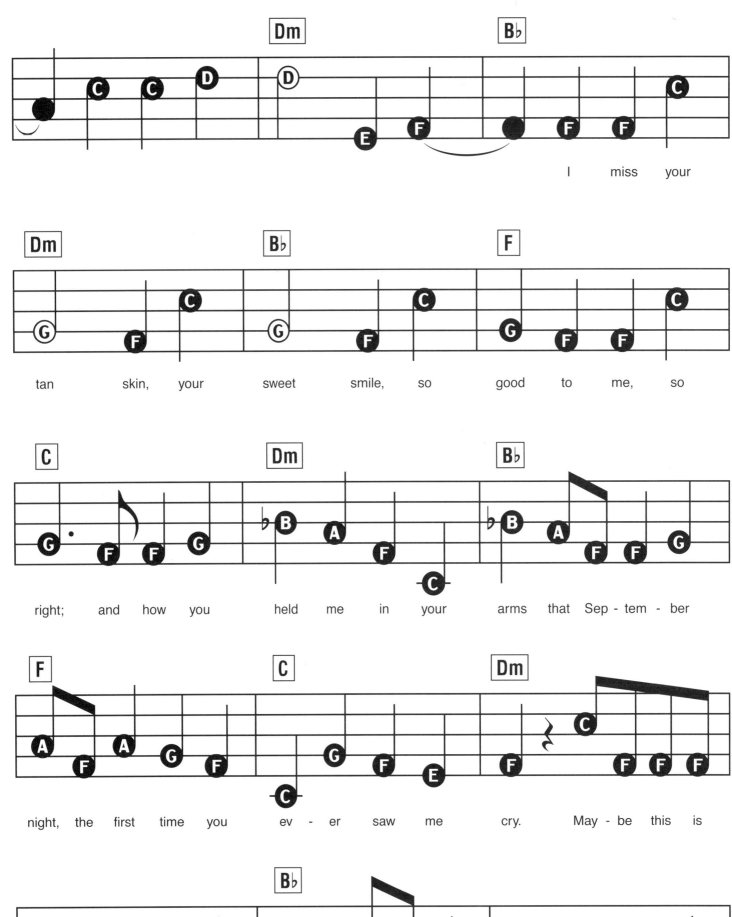

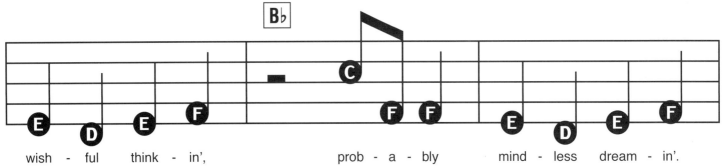

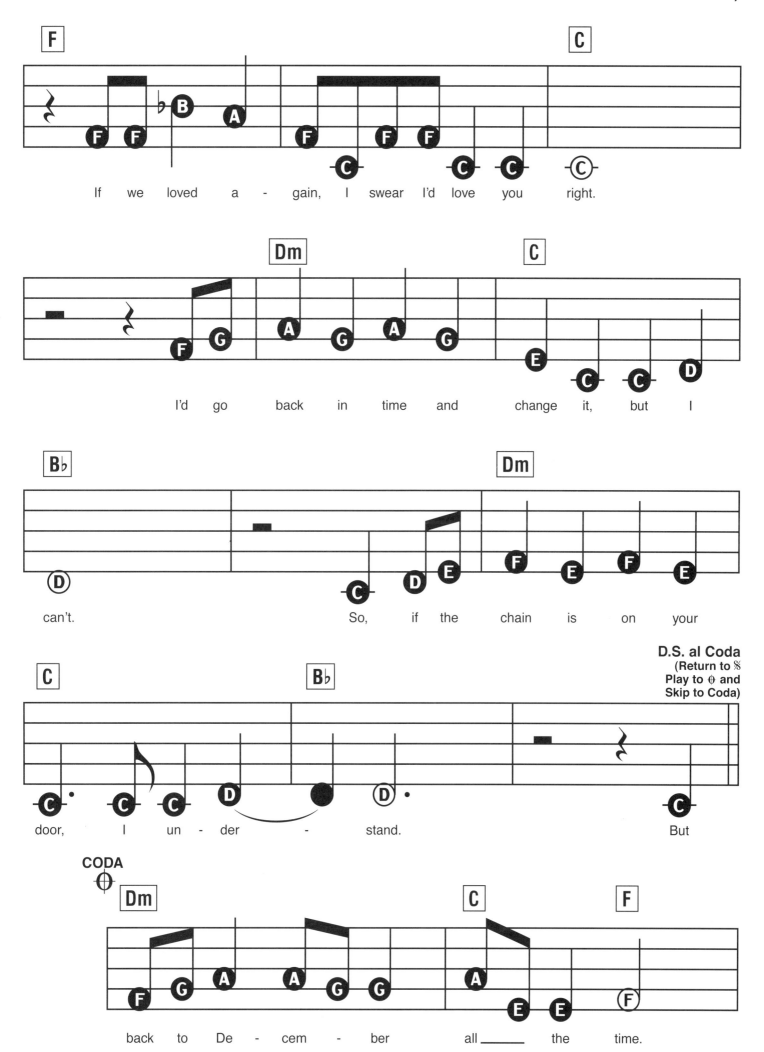

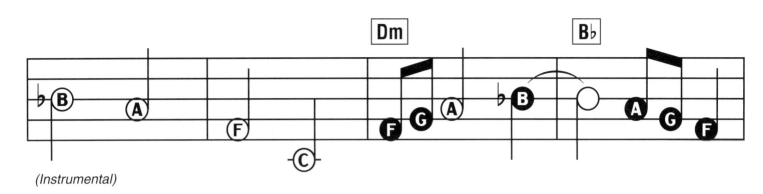

(Instrumental)

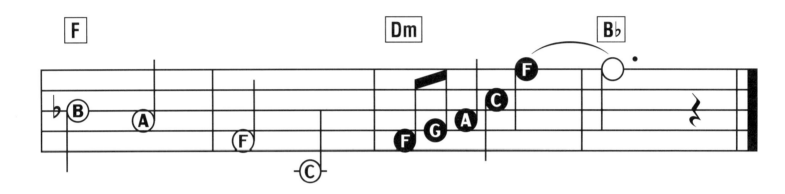

Additional Lyrics

2. These days I haven't been sleepin';
Stayin' up, playin' back myself leavin',
When your birthday passed and I didn't call.
Then I think about summer, all the beautiful times
I watched you laughin' from the passenger side
And realized I loved you in the fall.
And then the cold came, the dark days
When fear crept into my mind.
You gave me all your love and
All I gave you was goodbye.

So, this is me swallowin' my pride…

Enchanted

Registration 1
Rhythm: 8-Beat or Rock

Words and Music by
Taylor Swift

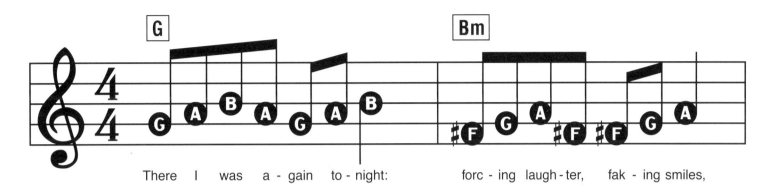

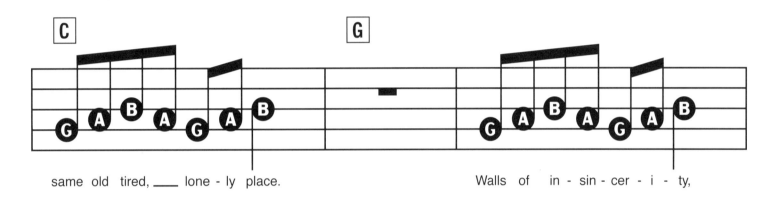

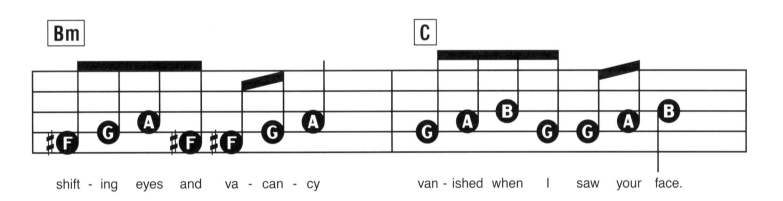

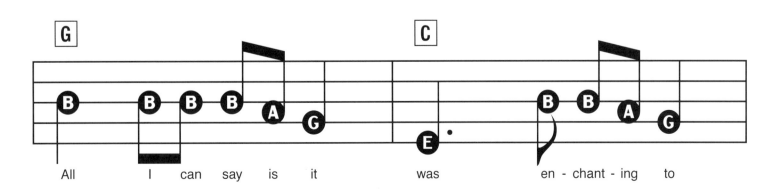

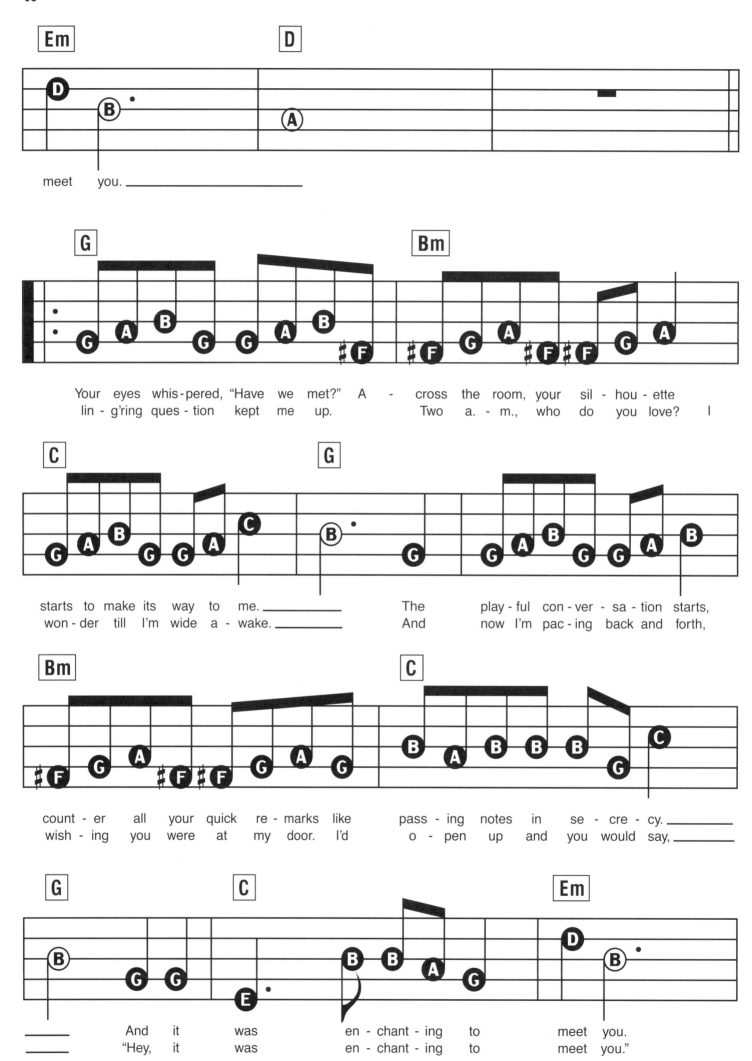

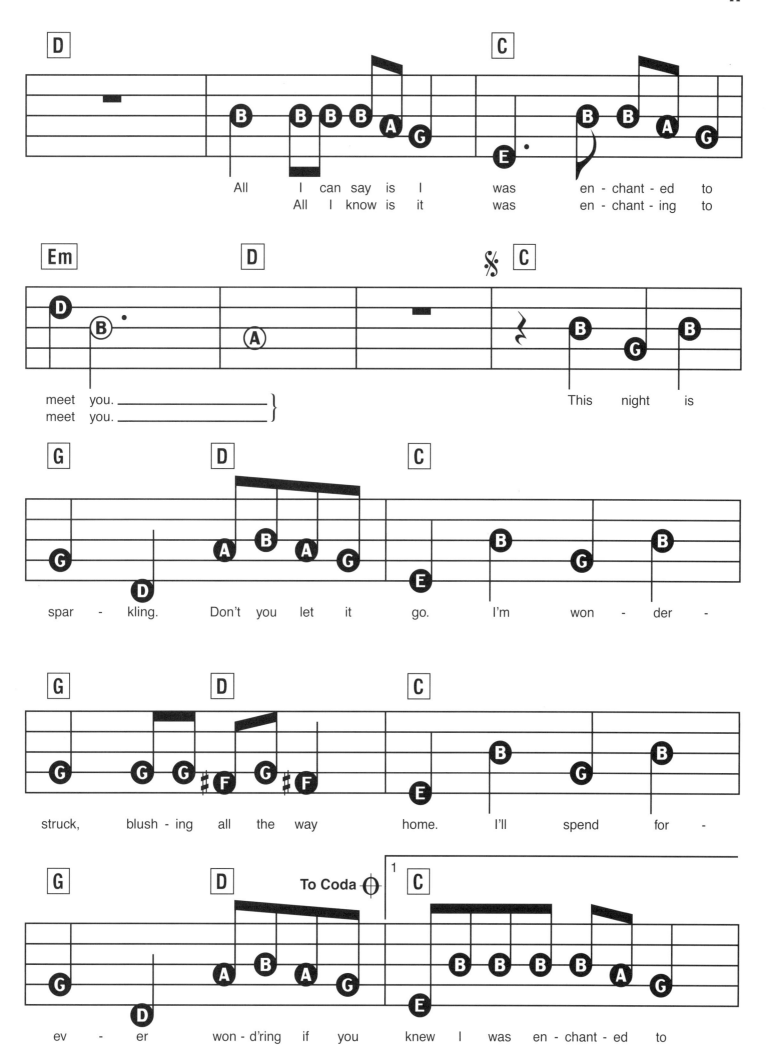

12

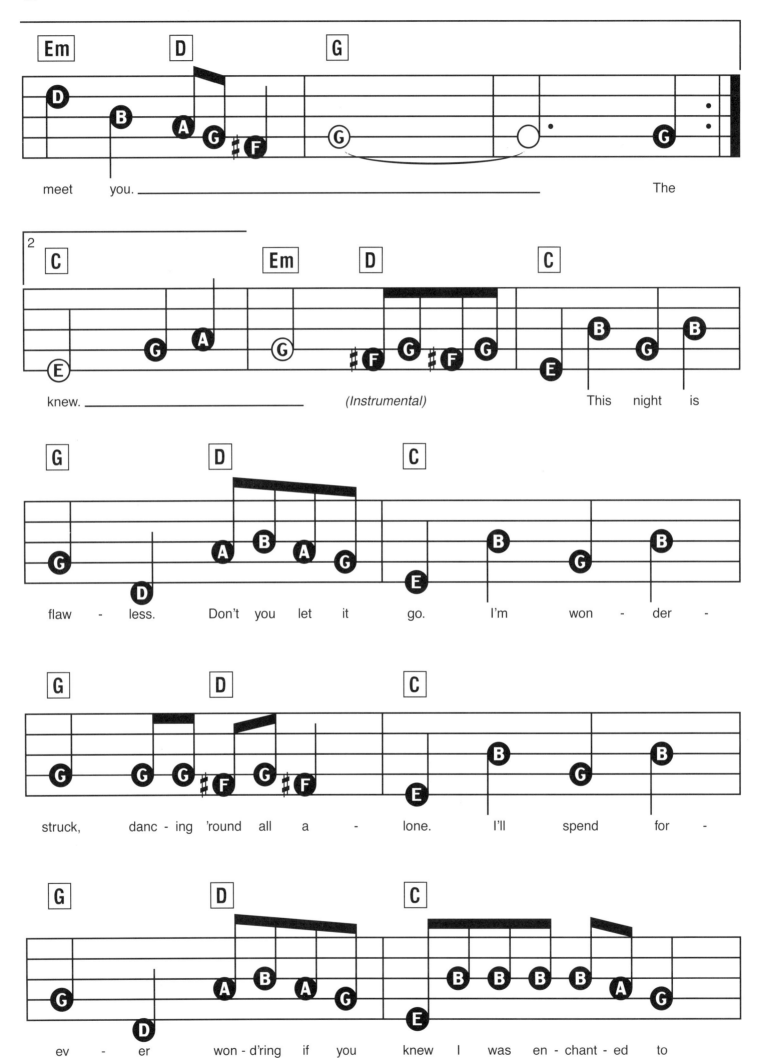

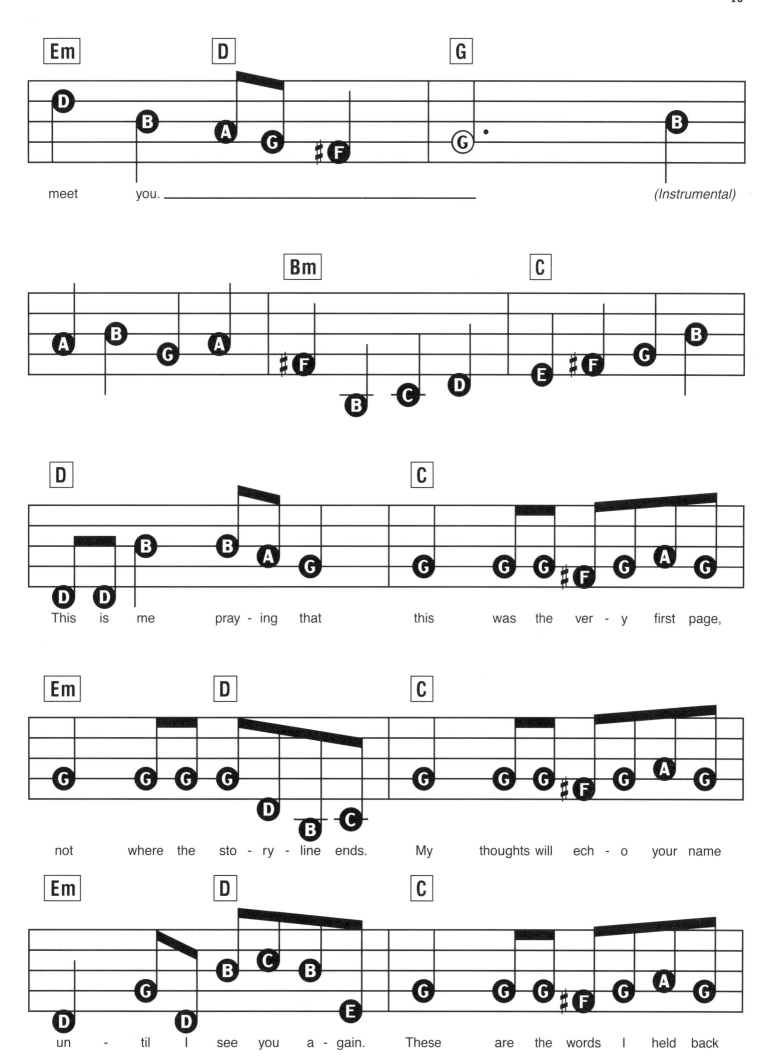

14

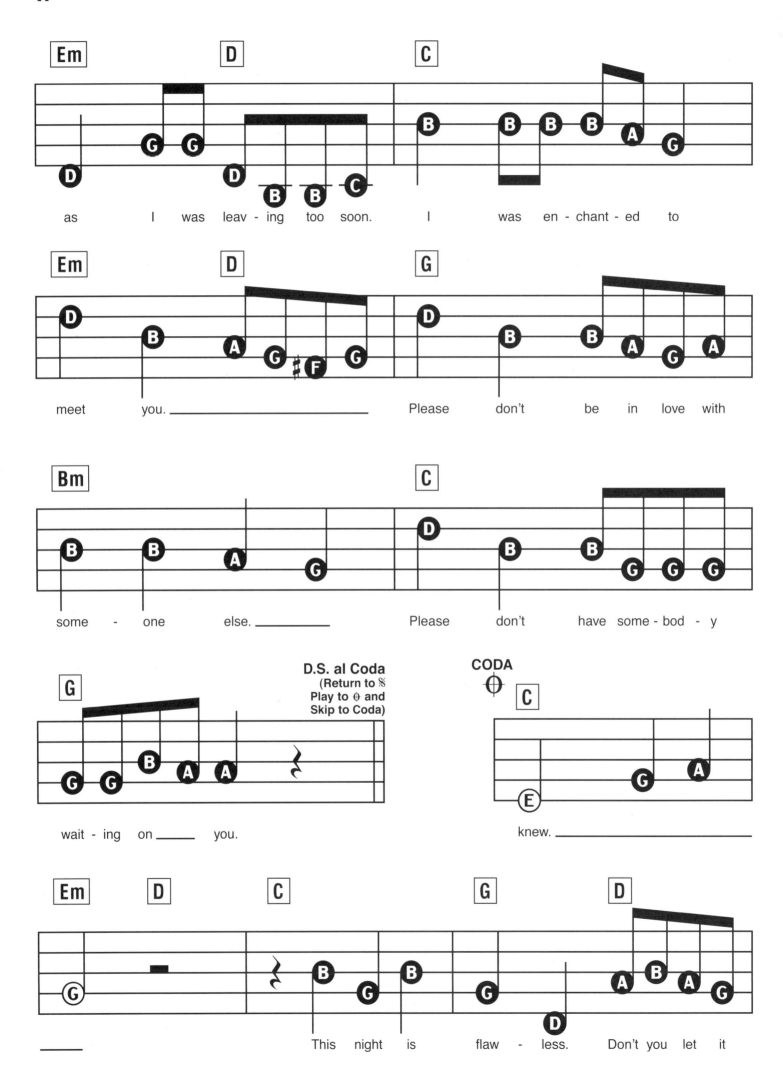

15

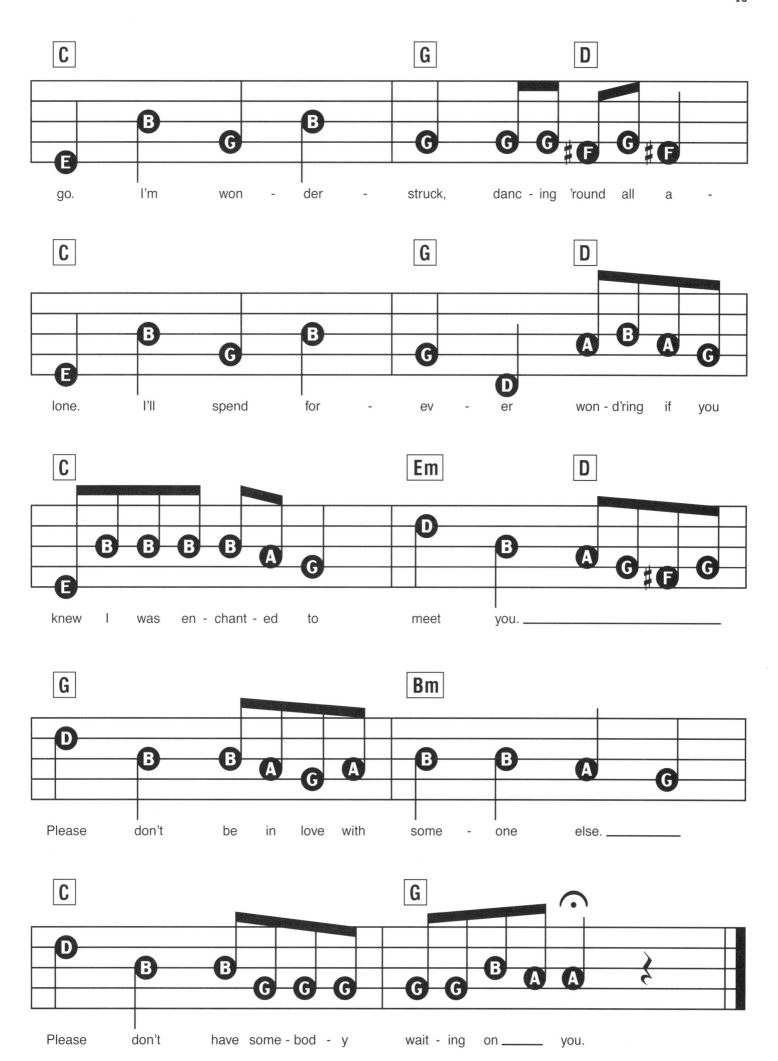

Begin Again

Registration 3
Rhythm: Rock or Country Pop

Words and Music by
Taylor Swift

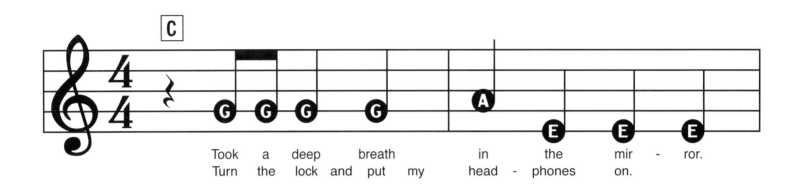

Took a deep breath in the mir - ror.
Turn the lock and put my head - phones on.

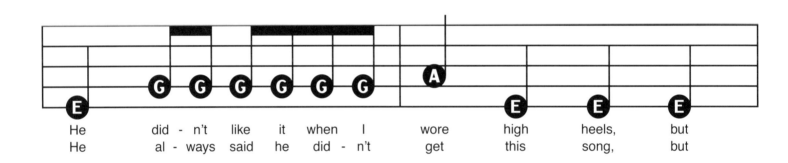

He did - n't like it when I wore high heels, but
He al - ways said he did - n't get this song, but

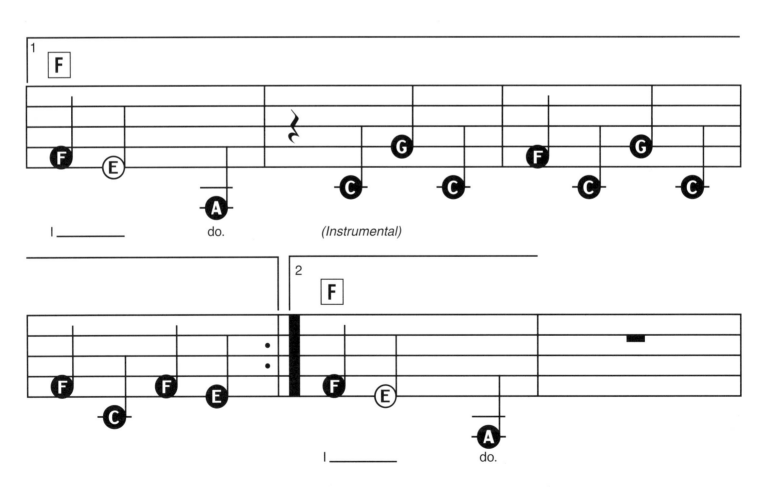

I _____ do. (Instrumental)

I _____ do.

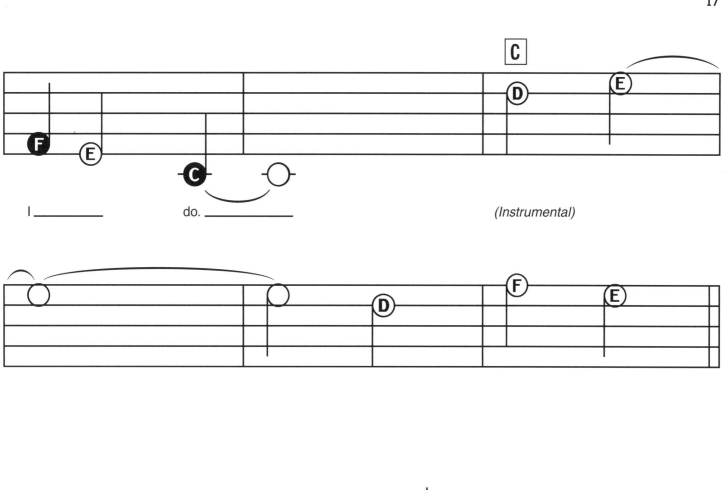

I _____ do. _____ (Instrumental)

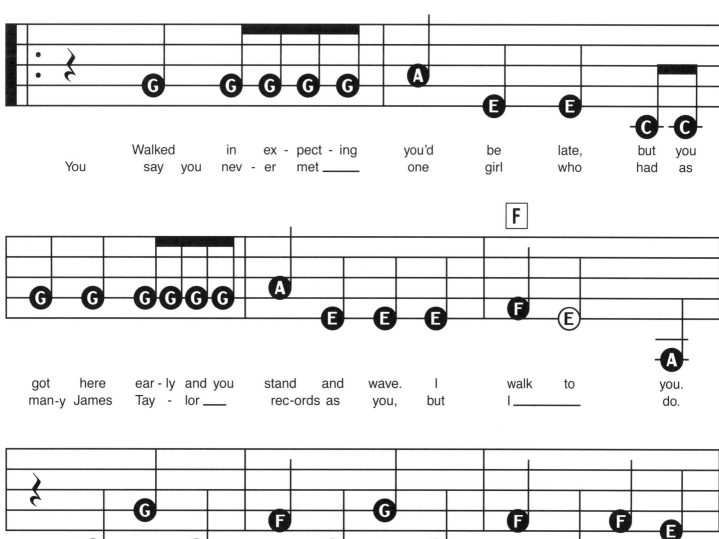

Walked in ex‑pect‑ing you'd be late, but you
You say you nev‑er met _____ one girl who had as

got here ear‑ly and you stand and wave. I walk to you.
man‑y James Tay‑lor _____ rec‑ords as you, but I _____ do.

(Instrumental)

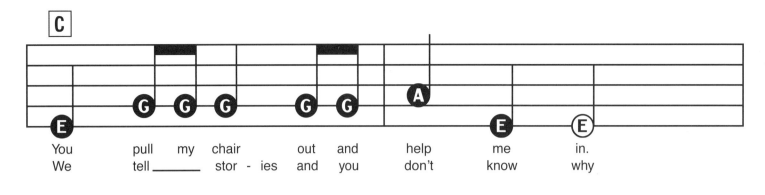

You pull my chair out and help me in.
We tell _____ stor - ies and you don't know why

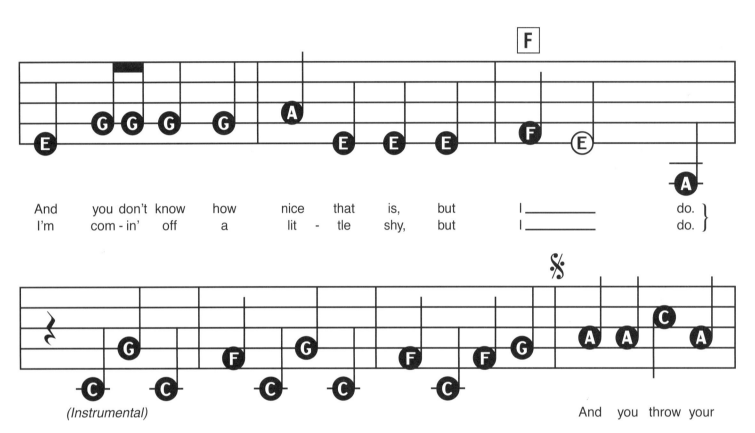

And you don't know how nice that is, but I _____ do. }
I'm com - in' off a lit - tle shy, but I _____ do. }

(Instrumental)

And you throw your

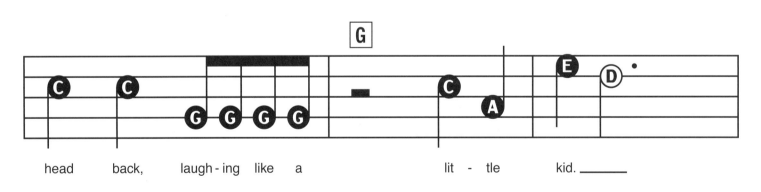

head back, laugh - ing like a lit - tle kid. _____

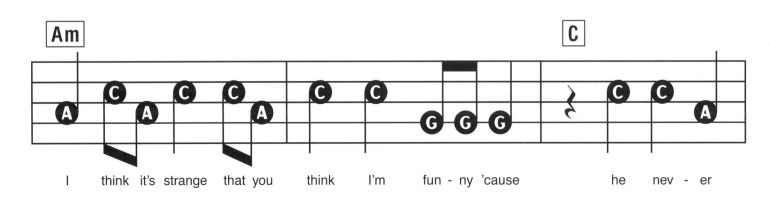

I think it's strange that you think I'm fun - ny 'cause he nev - er

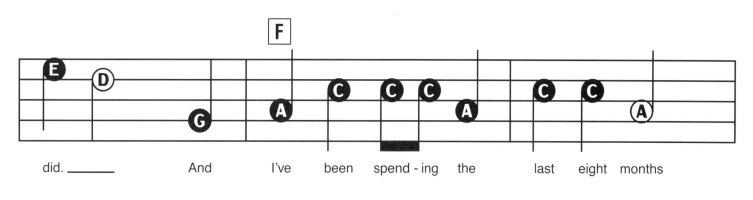

did. _____ And I've been spend - ing the last eight months

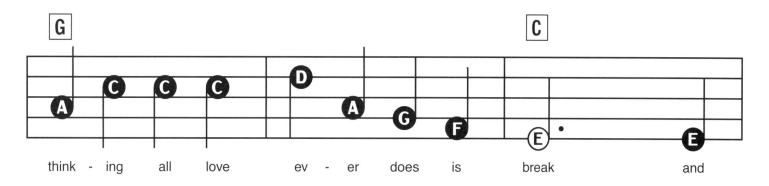

think - ing all love ev - er does is break and

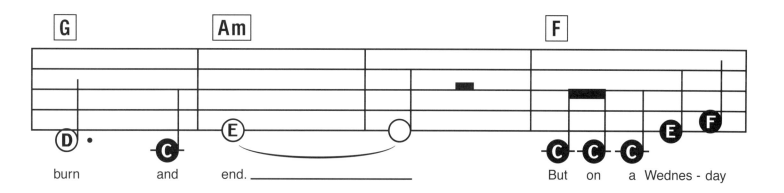

burn and end. _____ But on a Wednes - day

To Coda ⊕

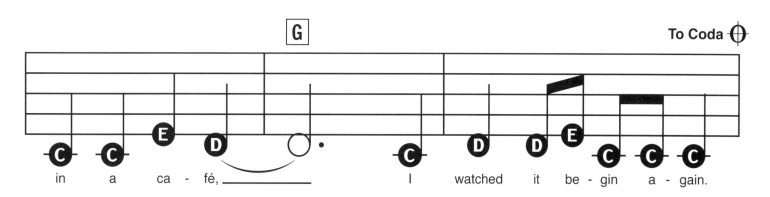

in a ca - fé, _____ I watched it be - gin a - gain.

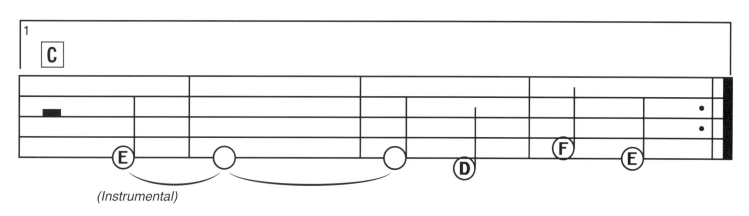

(Instrumental)

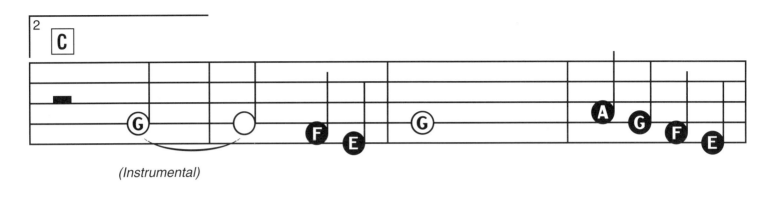

(Instrumental)

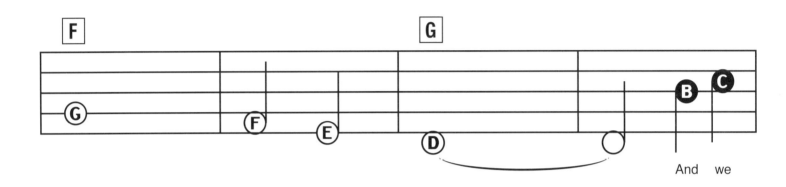

And we

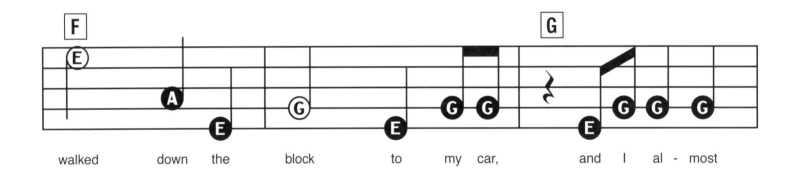

walked   down   the   block   to   my   car,   and   I   al - most

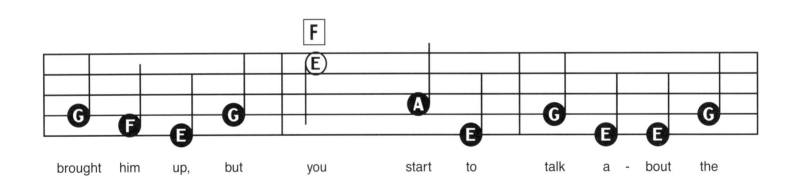

brought   him   up,   but   you   start   to   talk   a - bout   the

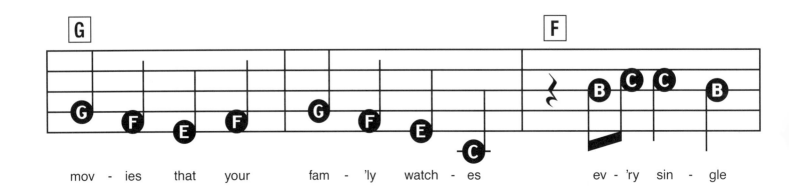

mov - ies   that   your   fam - 'ly   watch - es   ev - 'ry   sin - gle

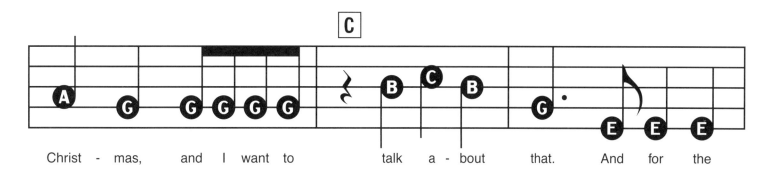

Christ - mas, and I want to talk a - bout that. And for the

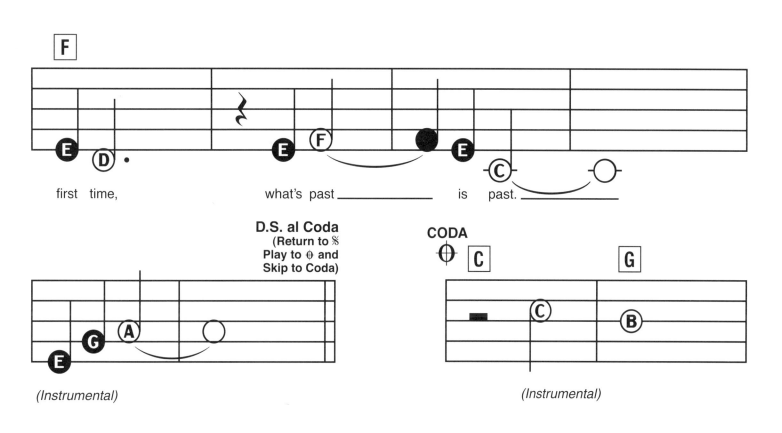

first time, what's past _____ is past. _____

D.S. al Coda
(Return to %
Play to ⊕ and
Skip to Coda)

(Instrumental)

CODA

(Instrumental)

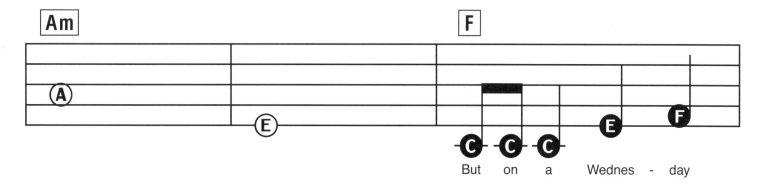

But on a Wednes - day

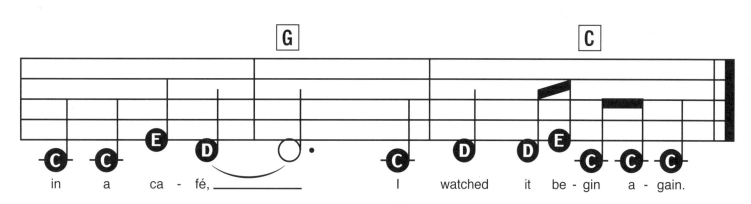

in a ca - fé, _____ I watched it be - gin a - gain.

I Almost Do

Registration 4
Rhythm: 8-Beat or Rock

Words and Music by
Taylor Swift

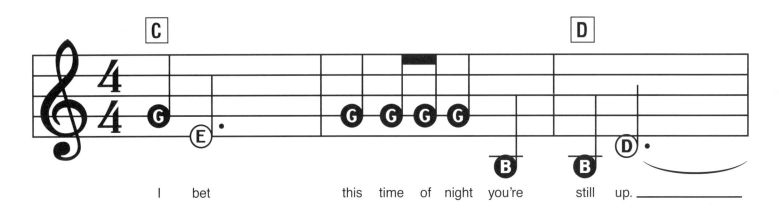

I bet this time of night you're still up. _____

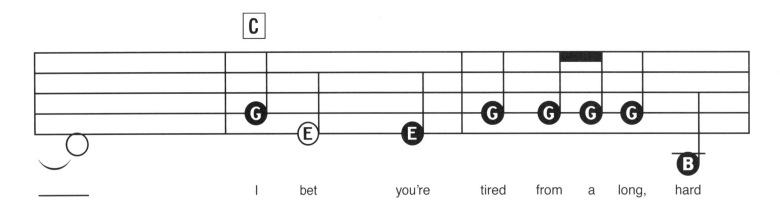

_____ I bet you're tired from a long, hard

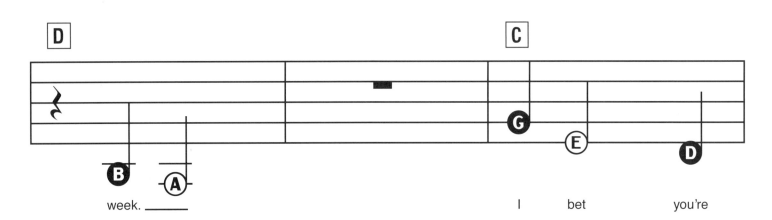

week. _____ I bet you're

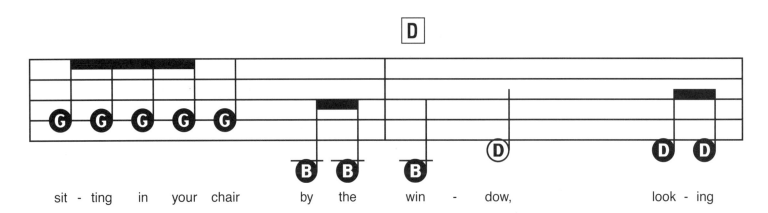

sit-ting in your chair by the win - dow, look - ing

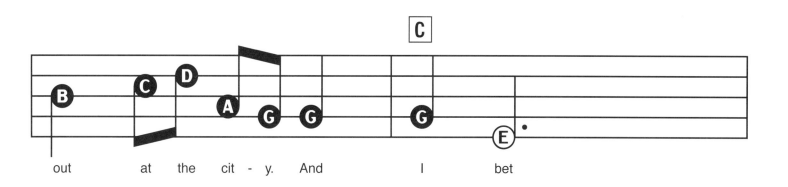

out   at   the   cit - y.   And   I   bet

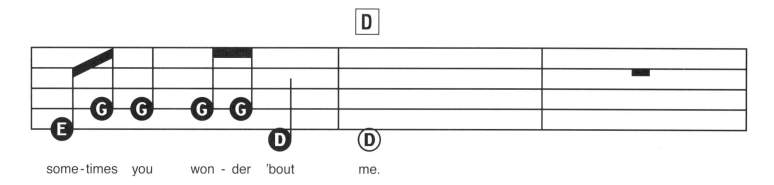

some-times   you   won - der   'bout   me.

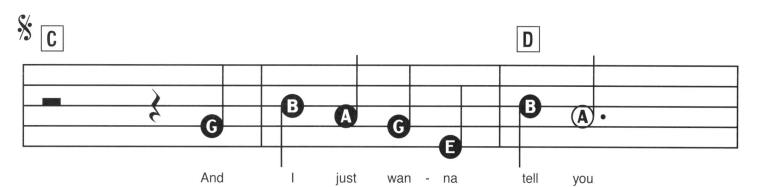

And   I   just   wan - na   tell   you

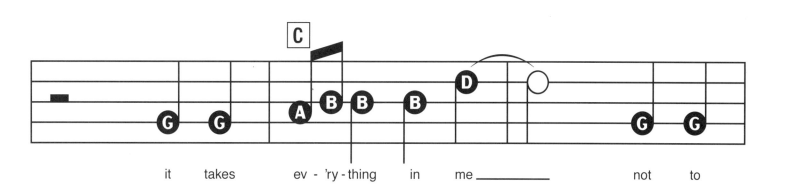

it   takes   ev - 'ry - thing   in   me _____   not   to

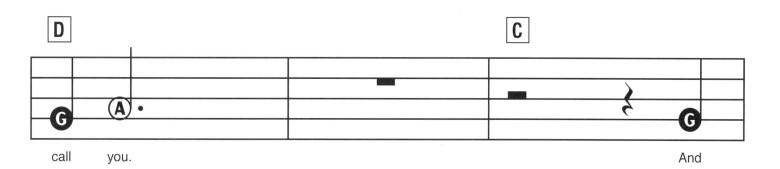

call   you.   And

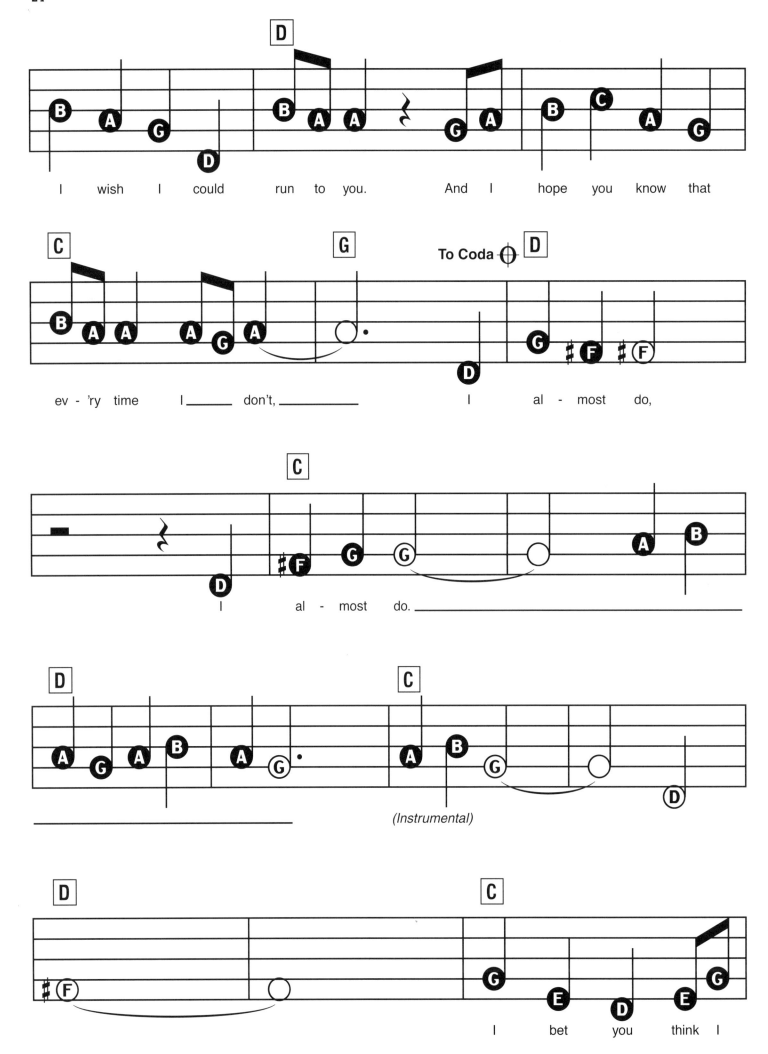

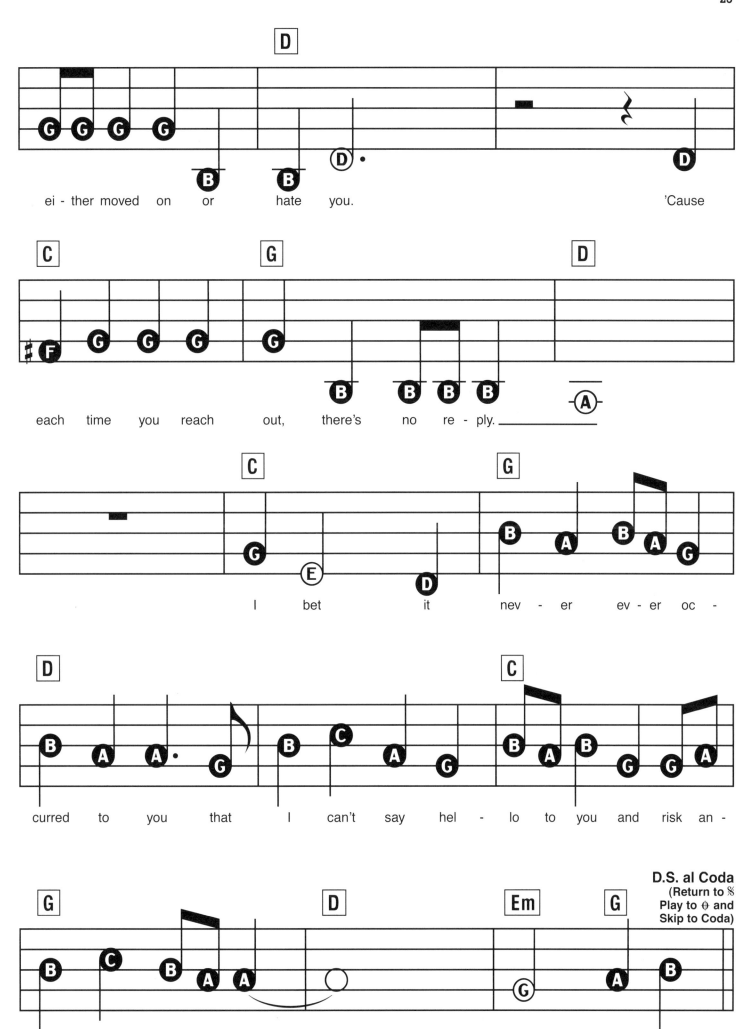

D

either moved on or hate you. 'Cause

C   G   D

each time you reach out, there's no re-ply. _____

C   G

I bet it nev-er ev-er oc-

D   C

curred to you that I can't say hel-lo to you and risk an-

G   D   Em   G

D.S. al Coda
(Return to 𝄋
Play to 𝄌 and
Skip to Coda)

oth-er good-bye. _____

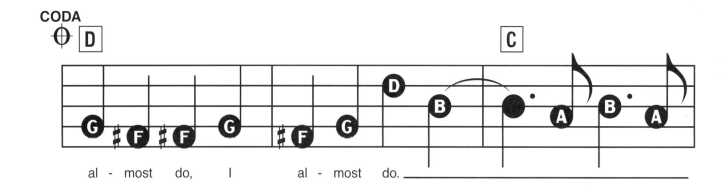

al - most do, I al - most do. _____

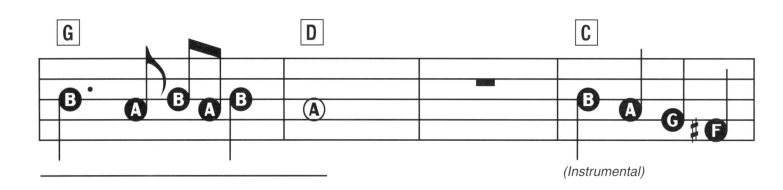

(Instrumental)

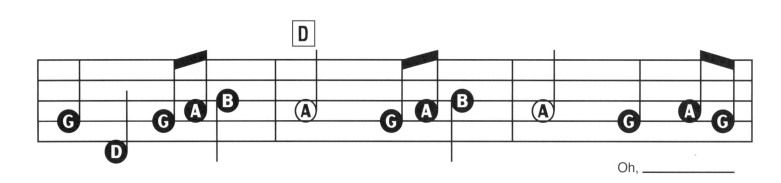

Oh, _____

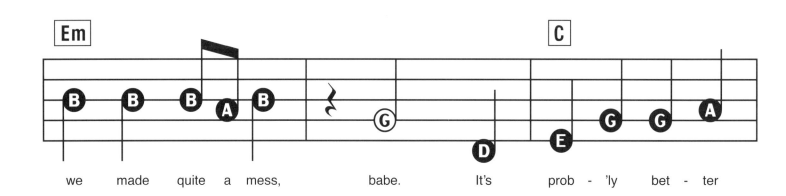

we made quite a mess, babe. It's prob - 'ly bet - ter

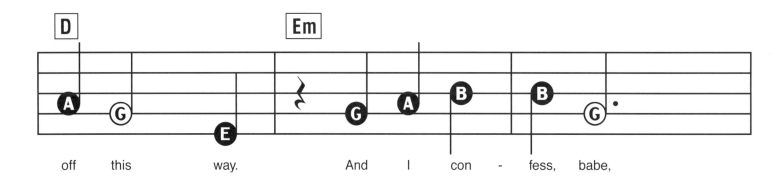

off this way. And I con - fess, babe,

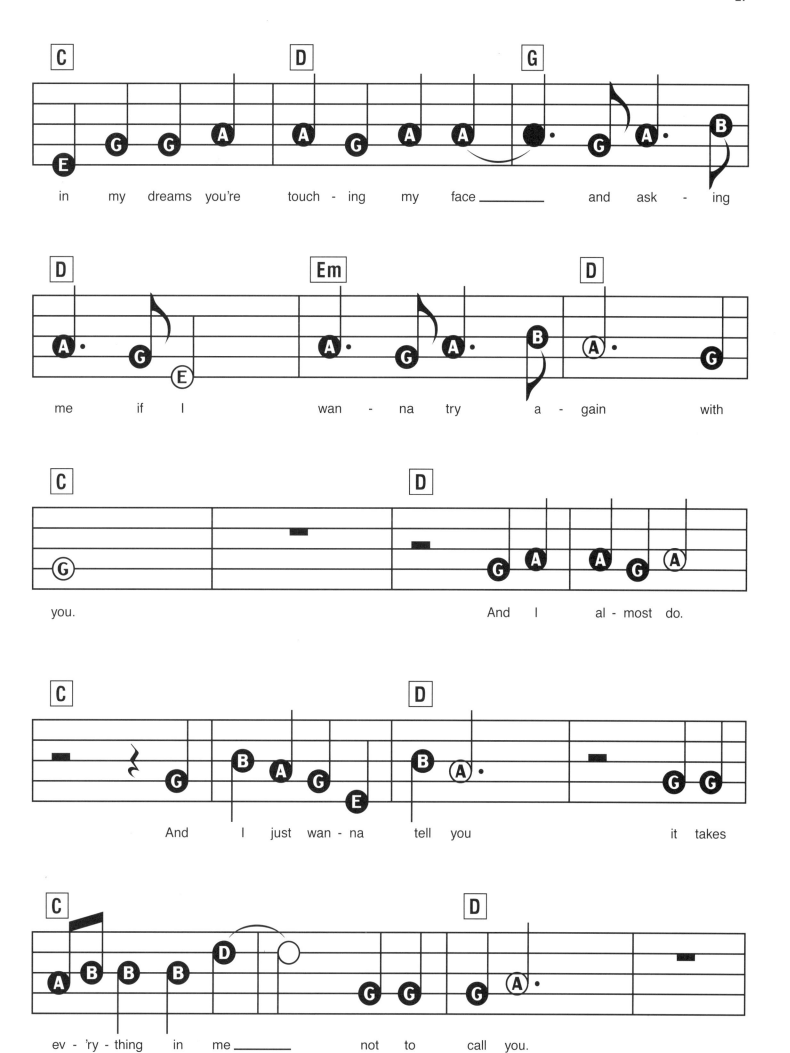

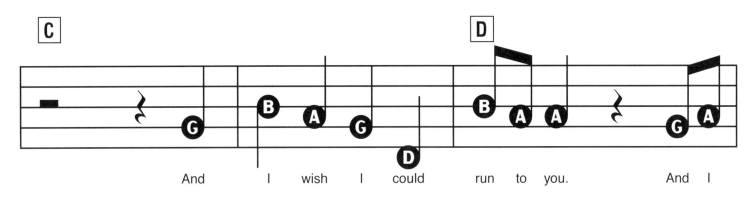

And I wish I could run to you. And I

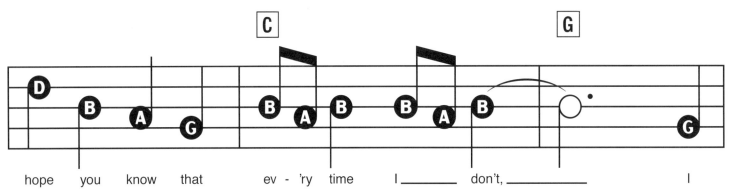

hope you know that ev - 'ry time I _____ don't, _____ I

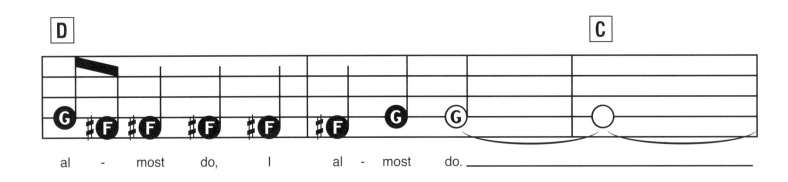

al - most do, I al - most do. _____

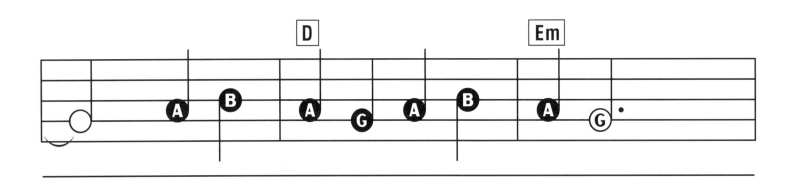

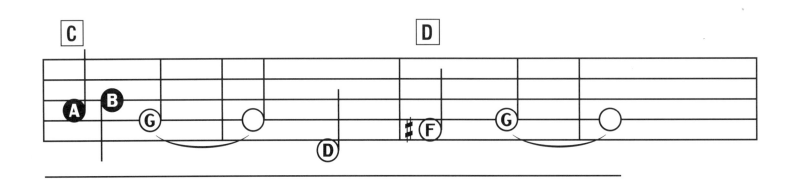

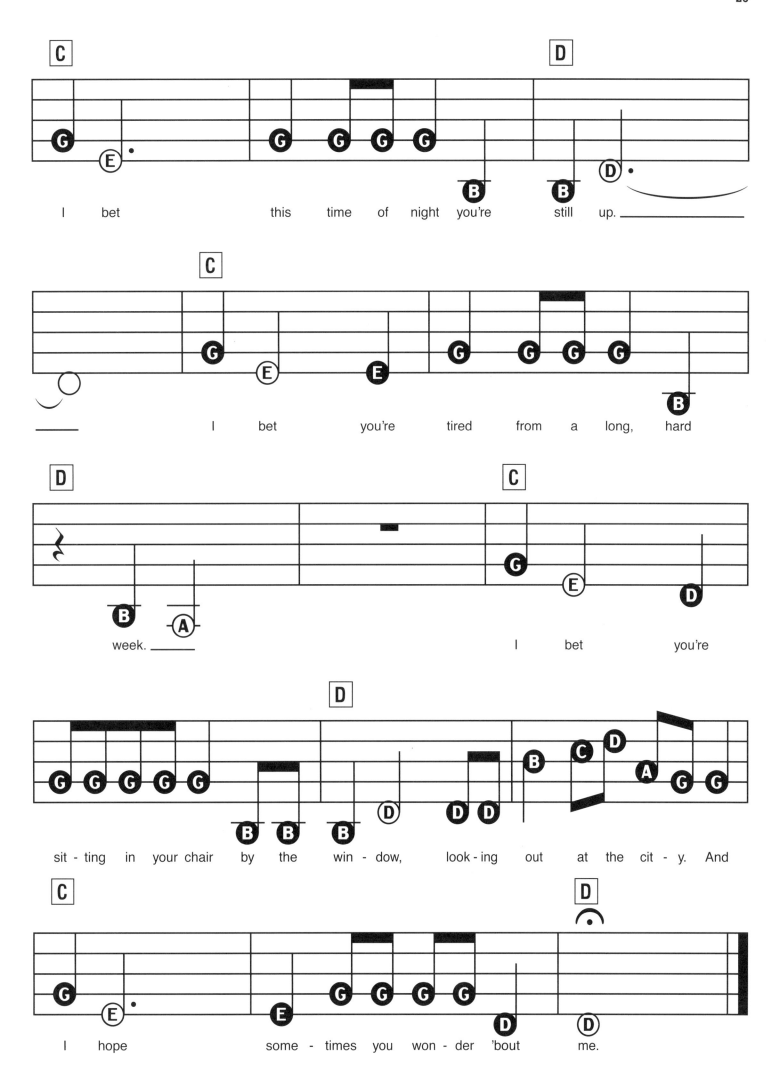

Mean

Registration 4
Rhythm: Bluegrass or Fox Trot

Words and Music by
Taylor Swift

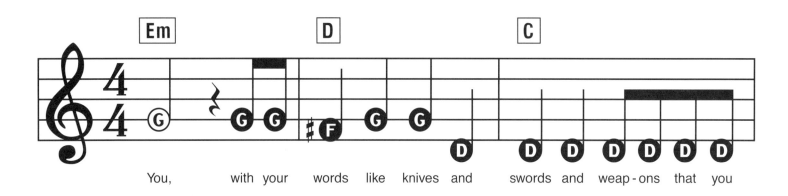

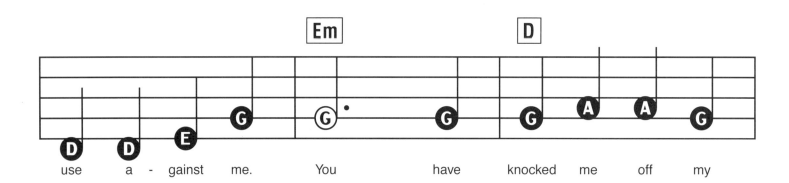

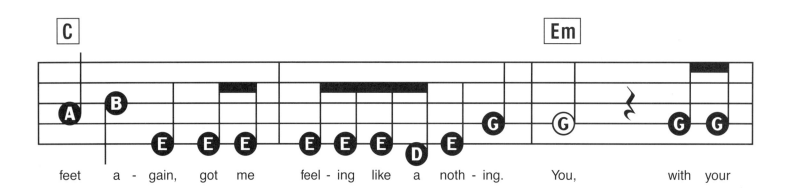

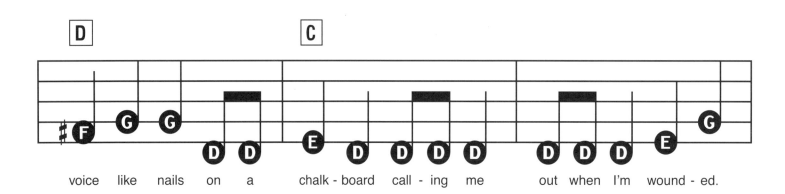

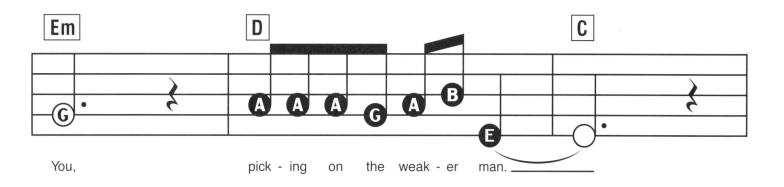

You, pick-ing on the weak-er man. _____

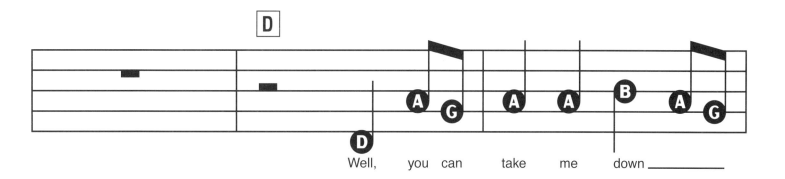

Well, you can take me down _____

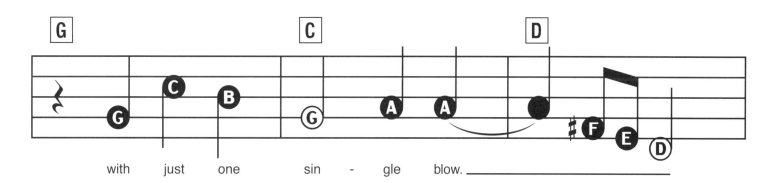

with just one sin - gle blow. _____

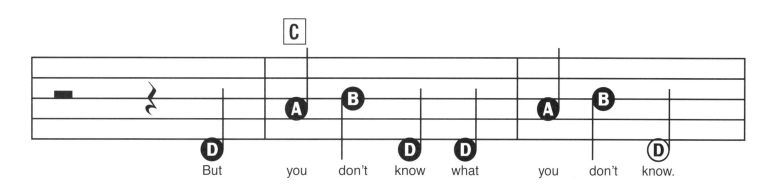

But you don't know what you don't know.

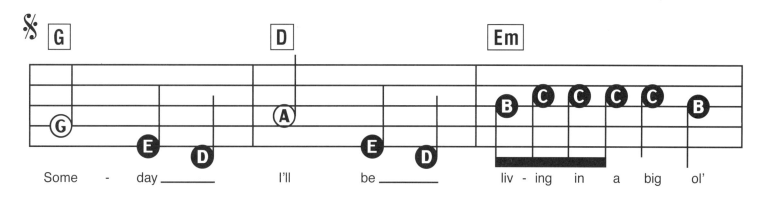

Some - day _____ I'll be _____ liv-ing in a big ol'

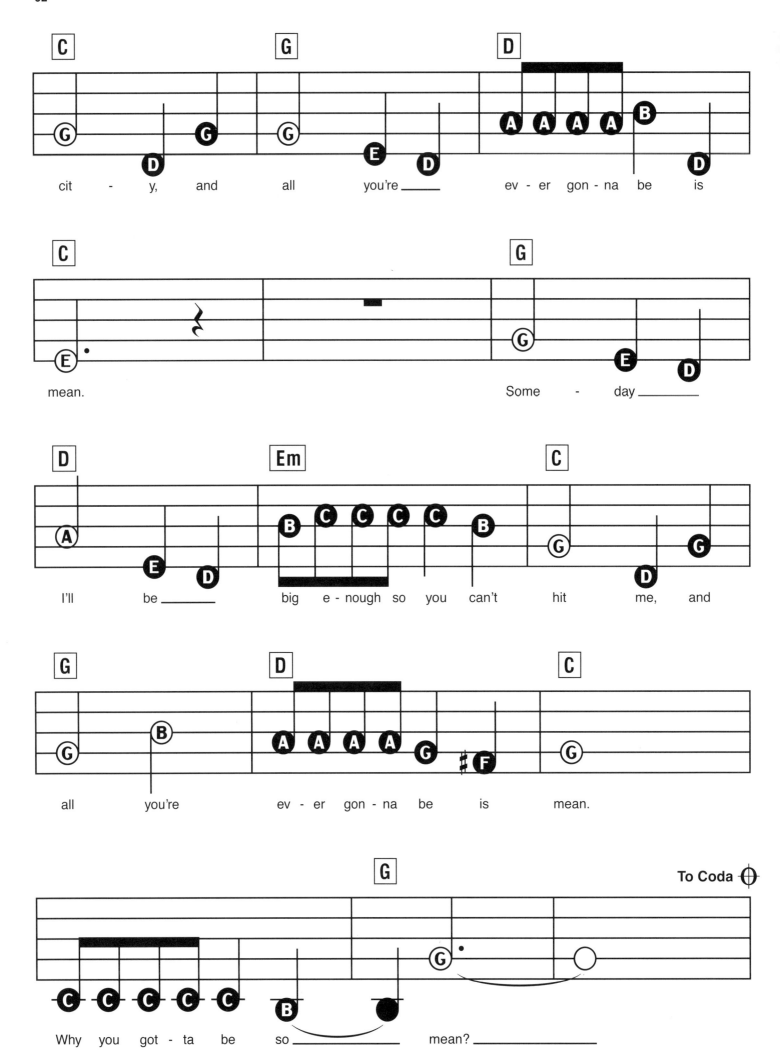

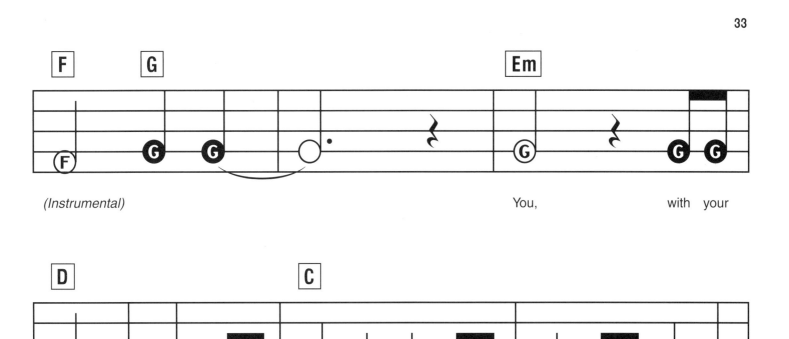

(Instrumental) You, with your

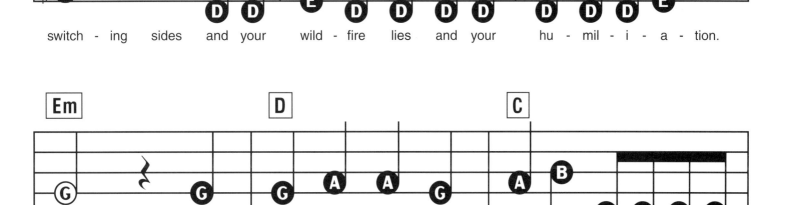

switch - ing sides and your wild - fire lies and your hu - mil - i - a - tion.

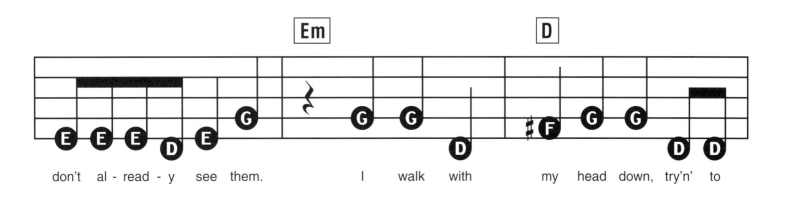

You have point - ed out my flaws a - gain, as if I

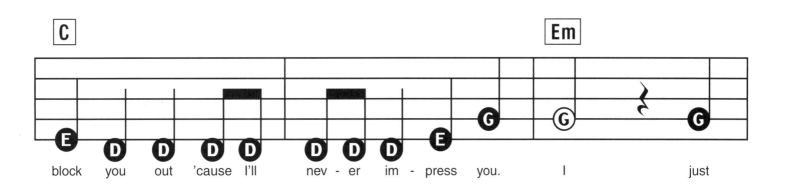

don't al - read - y see them. I walk with my head down, try'n' to

block you out 'cause I'll nev - er im - press you. I just

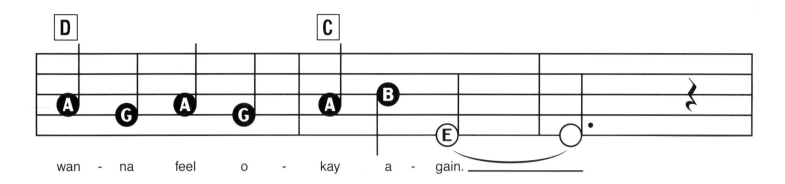

wan - na feel o - kay a - gain. _____

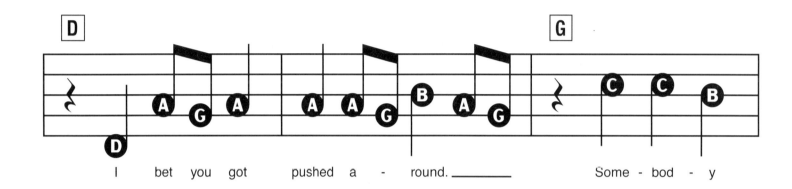

I bet you got pushed a - round. _____ Some - bod - y

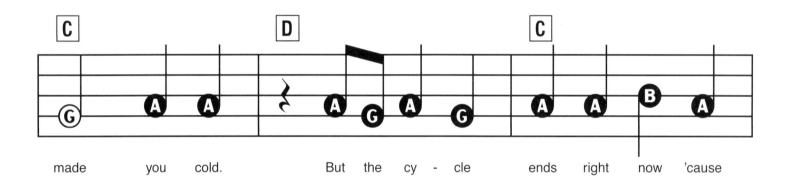

made you cold. But the cy - cle ends right now 'cause

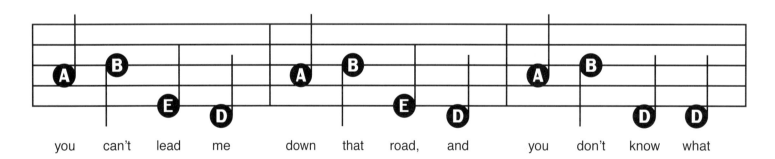

you can't lead me down that road, and you don't know what

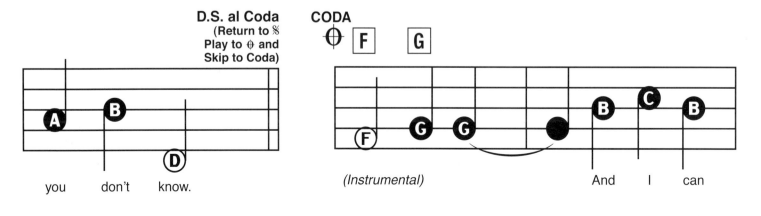

you don't know. (Instrumental) And I can

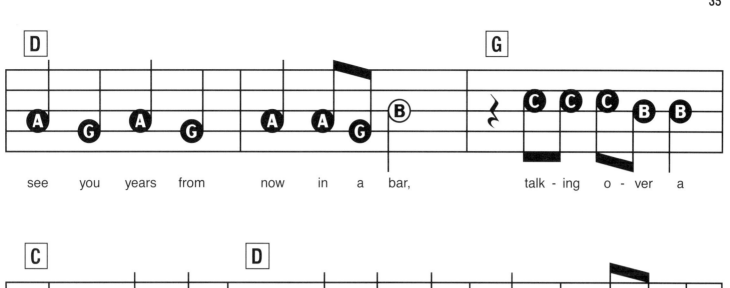

see you years from now in a bar, talk - ing o - ver a

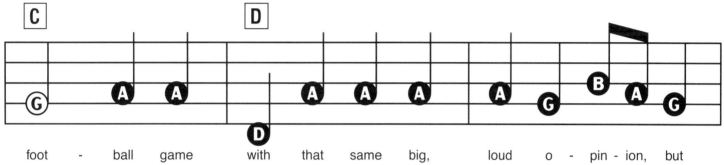

foot - ball game with that same big, loud o - pin - ion, but

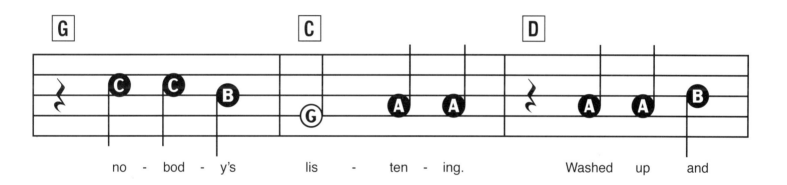

no - bod - y's lis - ten - ing. Washed up and

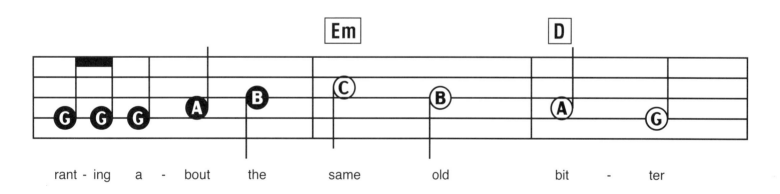

rant - ing a - bout the same old bit - ter

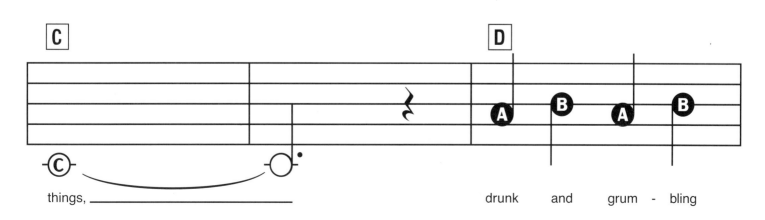

things, _____ drunk and grum - bling

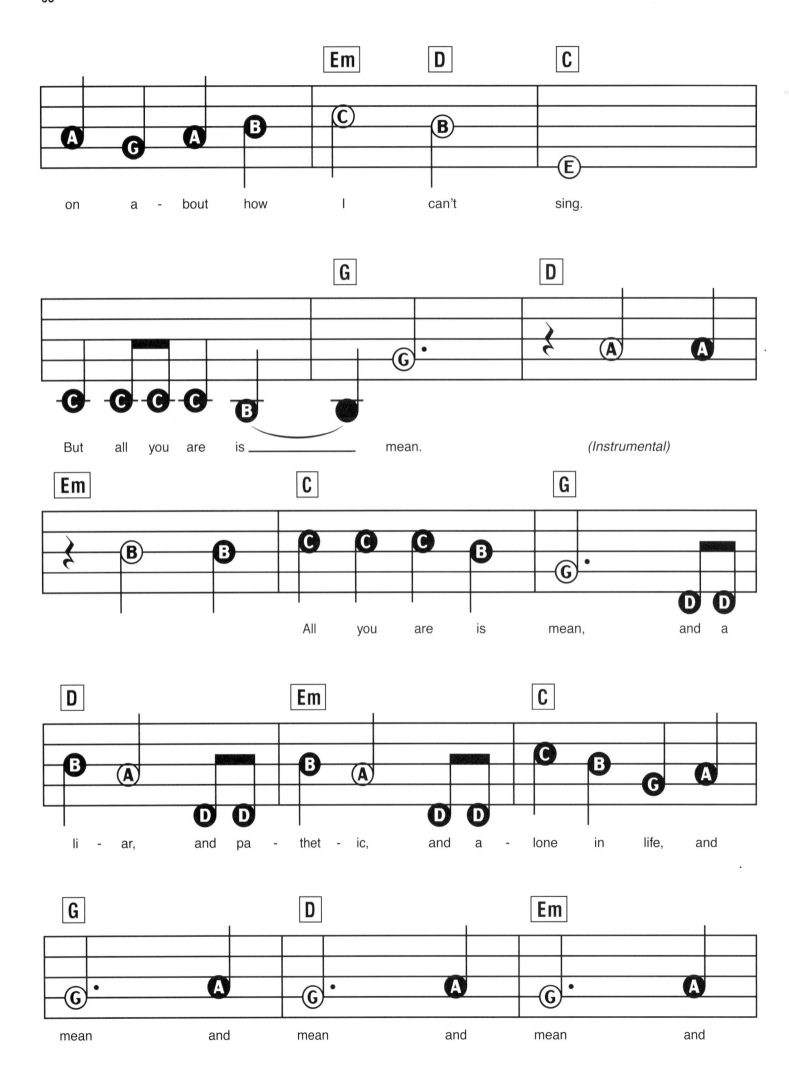

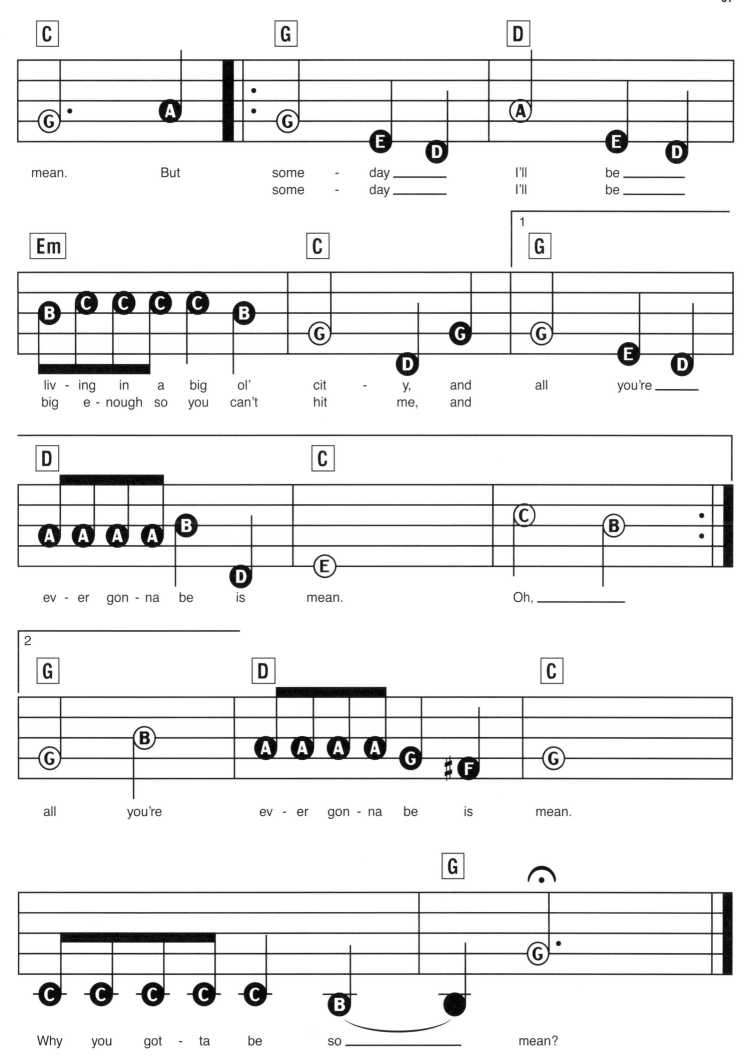

Mine

Registration 4
Rhythm: 8-Beat or Rock

Words and Music by
Taylor Swift

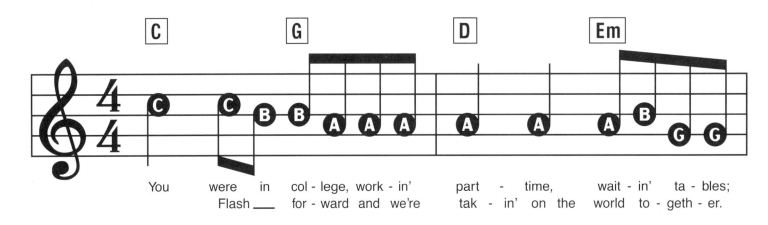

You were in col - lege, work - in' part - time, wait - in' ta - bles;
Flash ___ for - ward and we're tak - in' on the world to - geth - er.

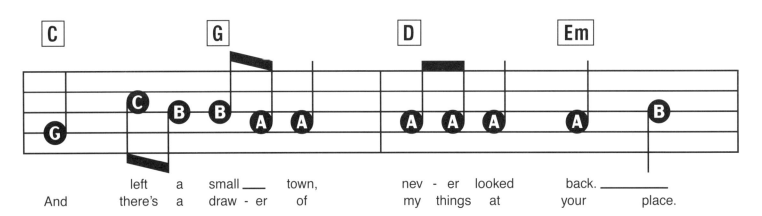

And left a small ___ town, nev - er looked back. _____
there's a draw - er of my things at your place.

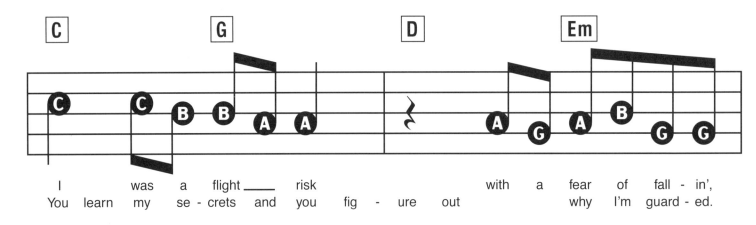

I was a flight ___ risk with a fear of fall - in',
You learn my se - crets and you fig - ure out why I'm guard - ed.

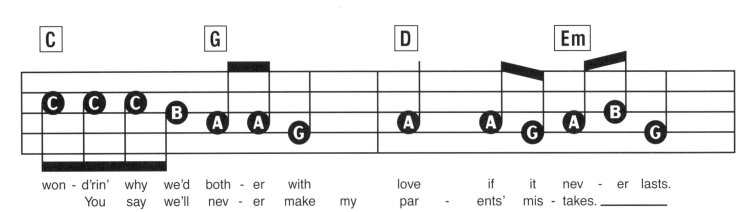

won - d'rin' why we'd both - er with love if it nev - er lasts.
You say we'll nev - er make my par - ents' mis - takes. _____

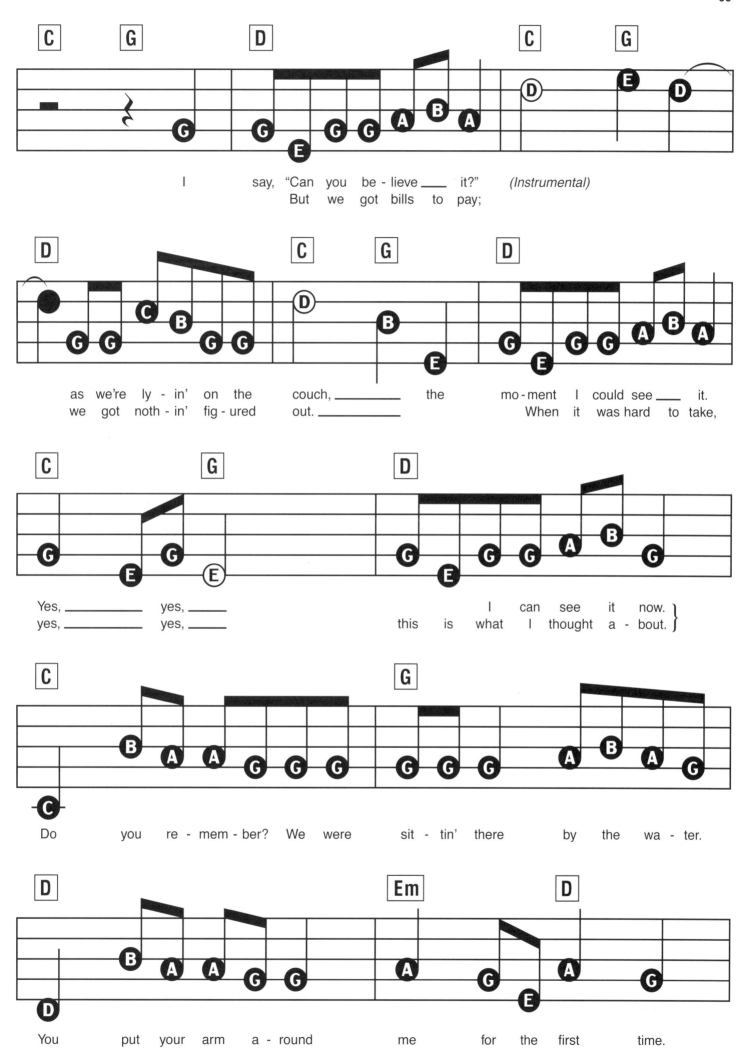

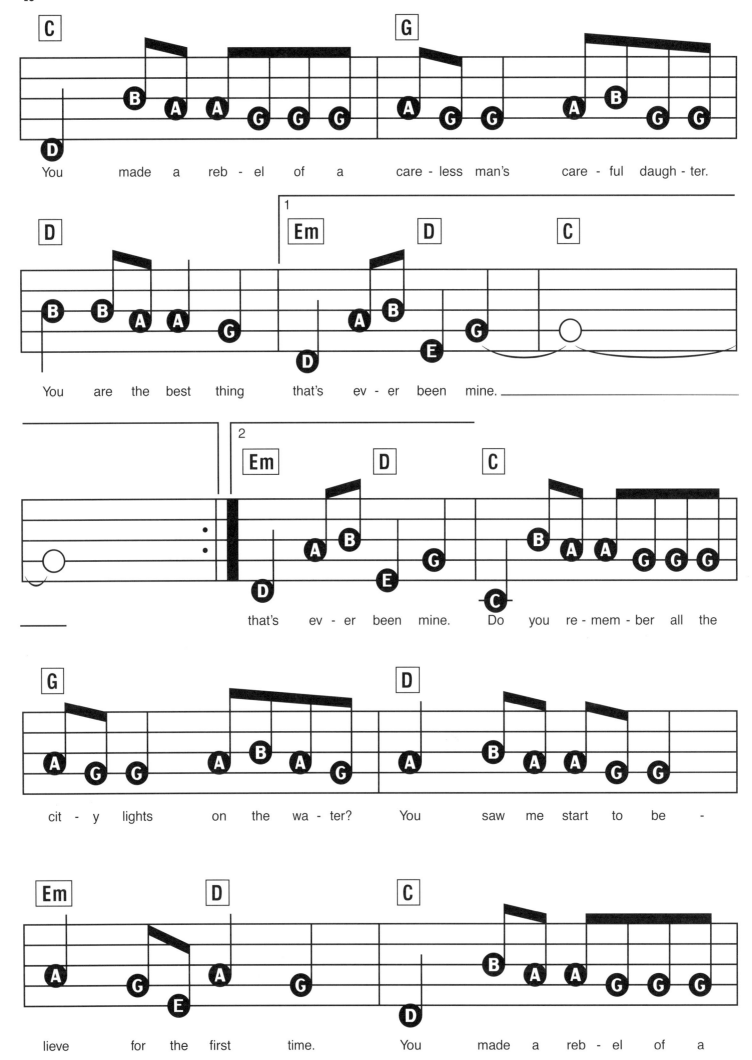

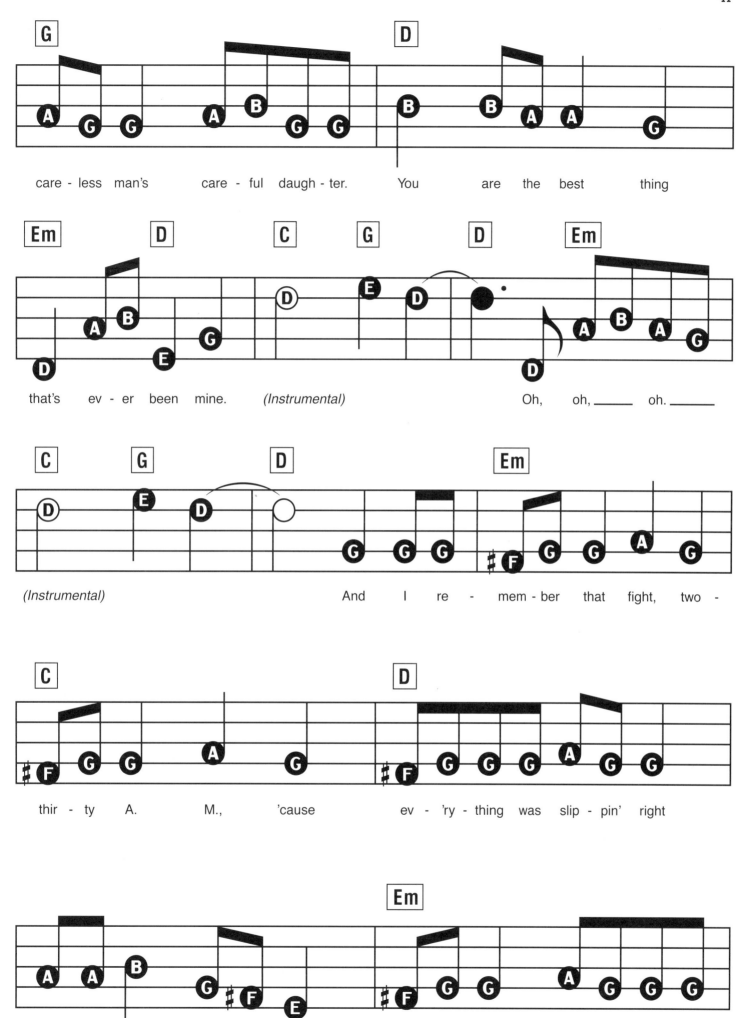

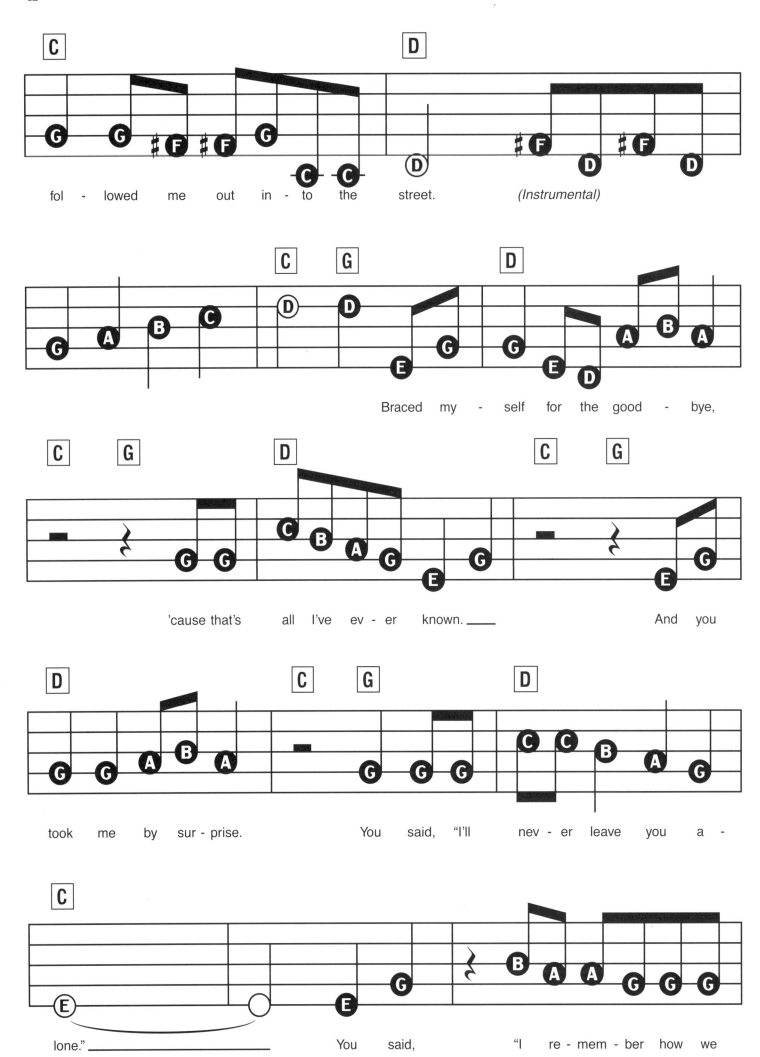

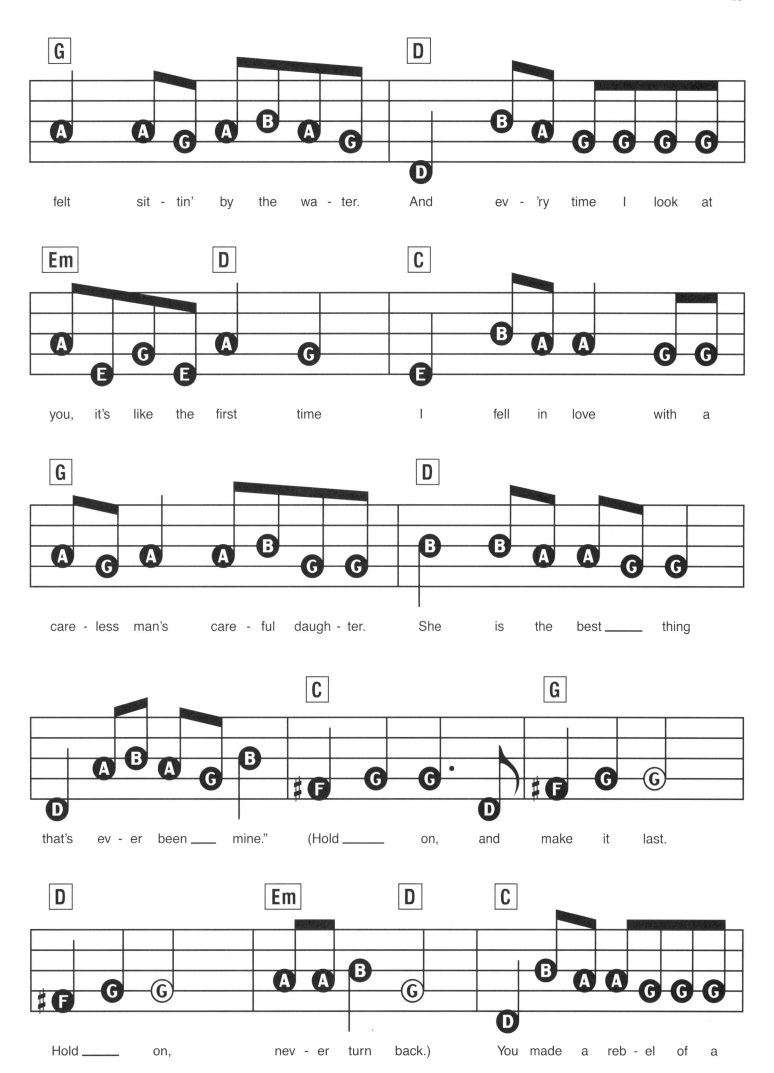

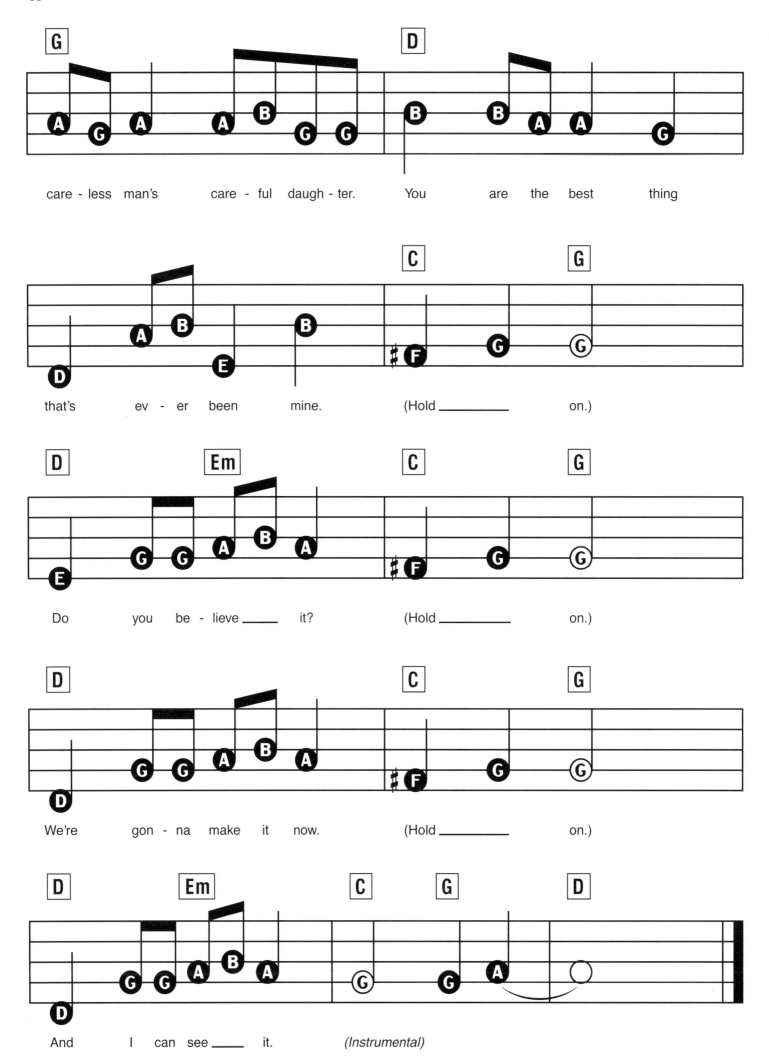

Red

Registration 4
Rhythm: Rock or Pop

Words and Music by
Taylor Swift

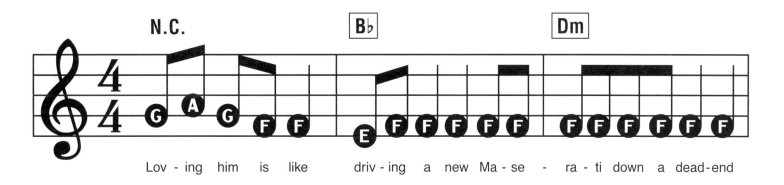

Lov - ing him is like driv - ing a new Ma - se - ra - ti down a dead-end

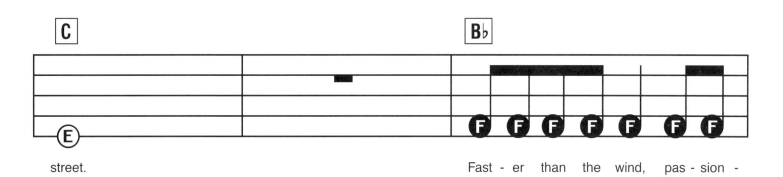

street.   Fast - er than the wind, pas - sion -

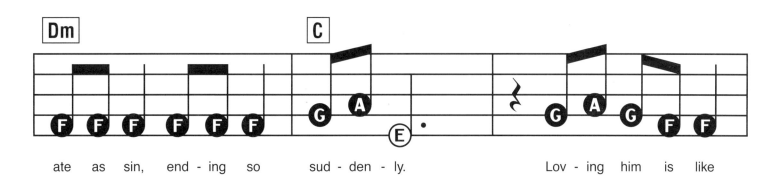

ate as sin, end - ing so sud - den - ly.   Lov - ing him is like

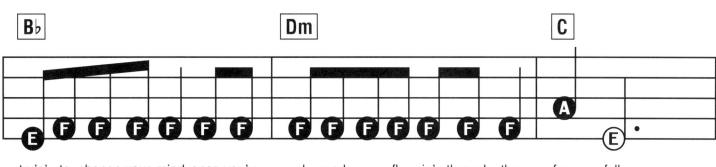

try'n' to change your mind once you're al - read - y fly - in' through the free fall,

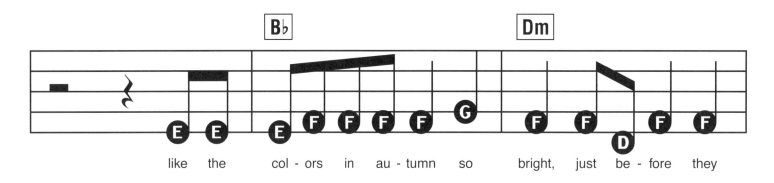

like the col - ors in au - tumn so bright, just be - fore they

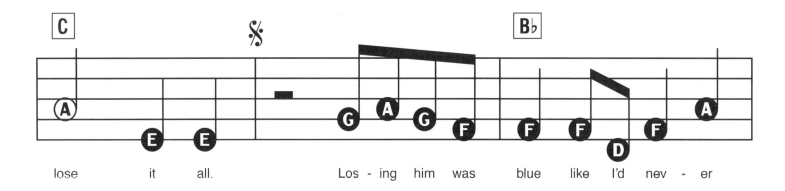

lose it all. Los - ing him was blue like I'd nev - er

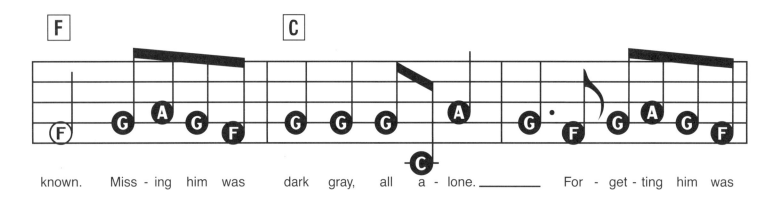

known. Miss - ing him was dark gray, all a - lone. _____ For - get - ting him was

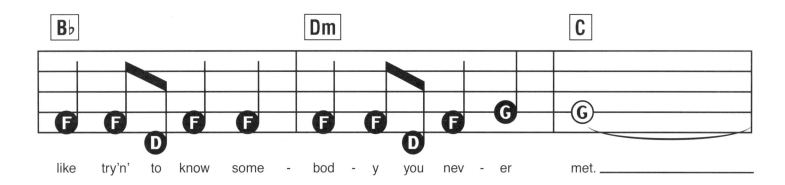

like try'n' to know some - bod - y you nev - er met. _____

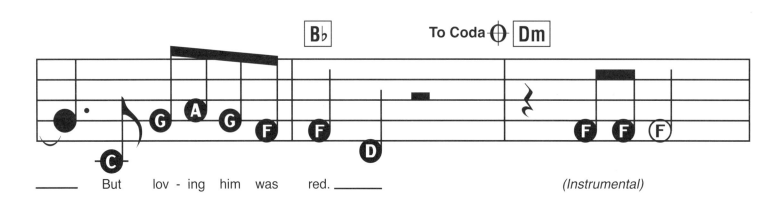

_____ But lov - ing him was red. _____ (Instrumental)

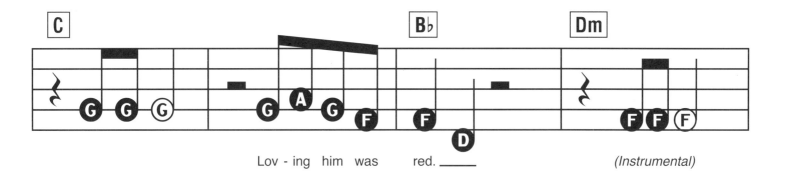

Lov - ing him was red. _____ *(Instrumental)*

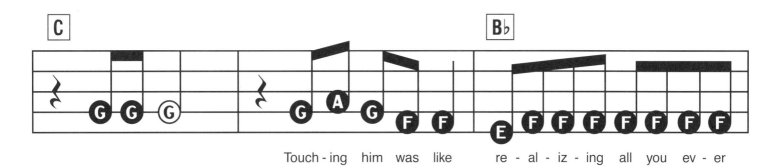

Touch - ing him was like re - al - iz - ing all you ev - er

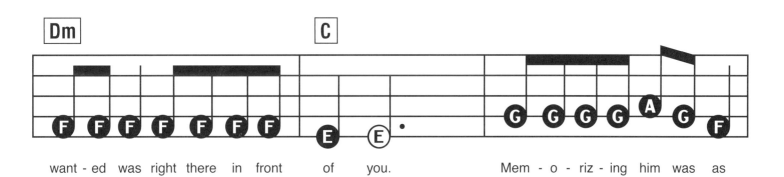

want - ed was right there in front of you. Mem - o - riz - ing him was as

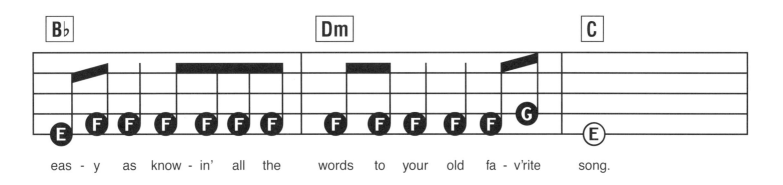

eas - y as know - in' all the words to your old fa - v'rite song.

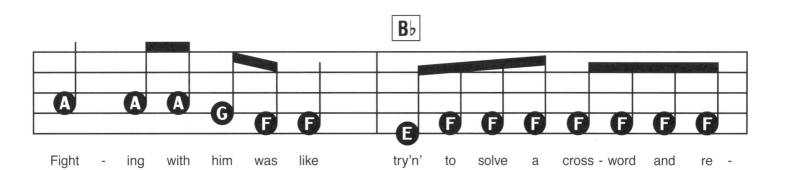

Fight - ing with him was like try'n' to solve a cross - word and re -

48

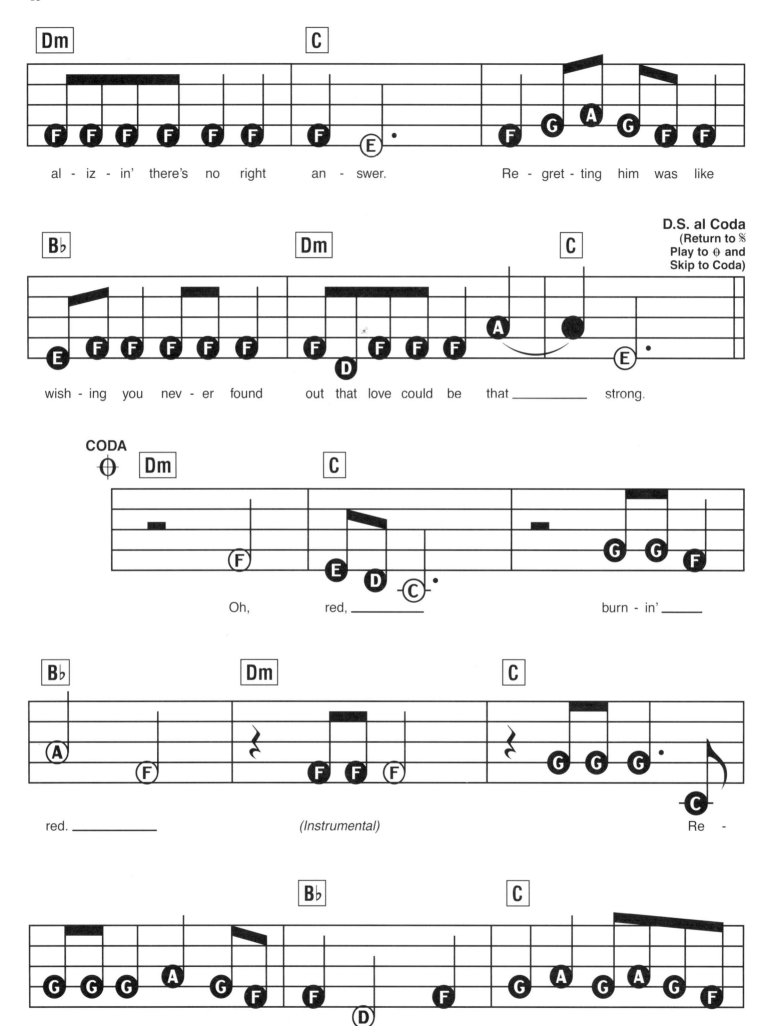

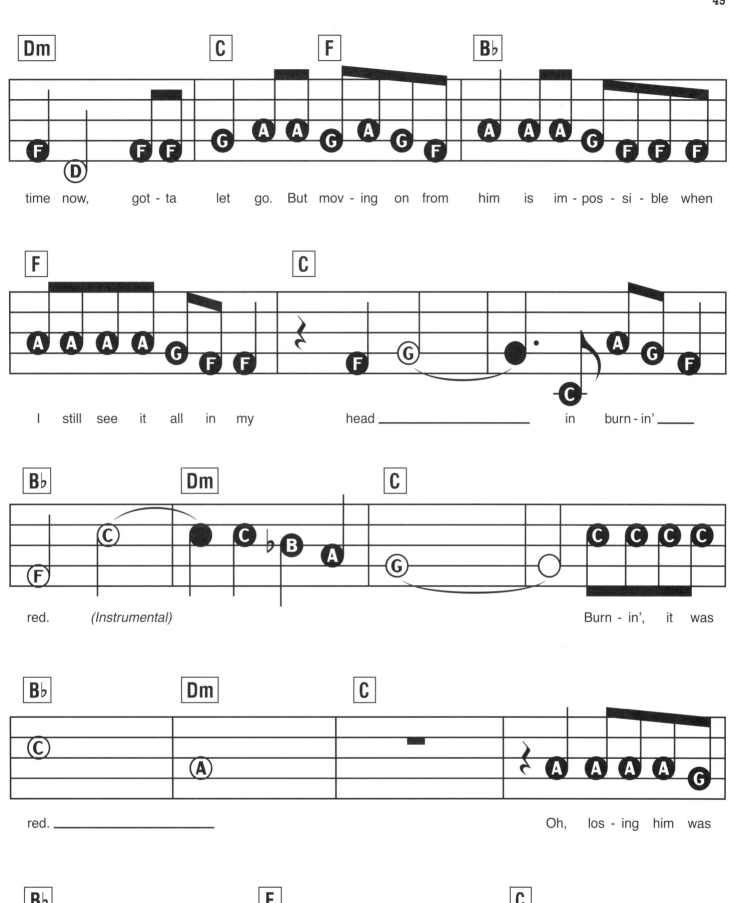

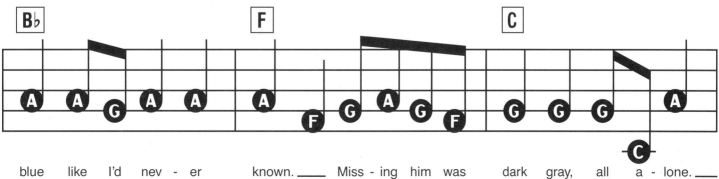

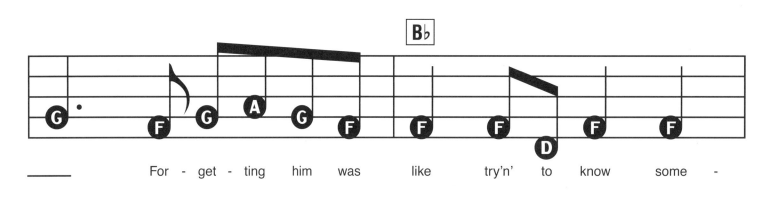

For - get - ting him was like try'n' to know some -

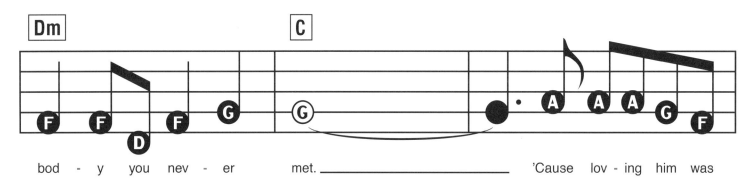

bod - y you nev - er met. _____ 'Cause lov - ing him was

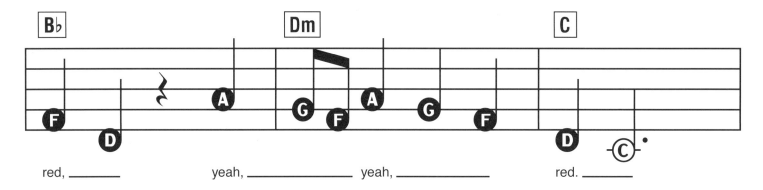

red, _____ yeah, _____ yeah, _____ red. _____

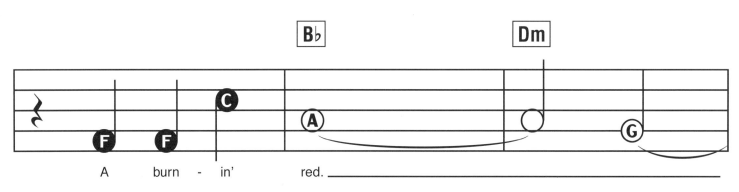

A burn - in' red. _____

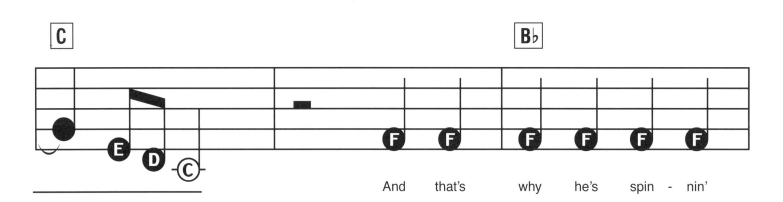

And that's why he's spin - nin'

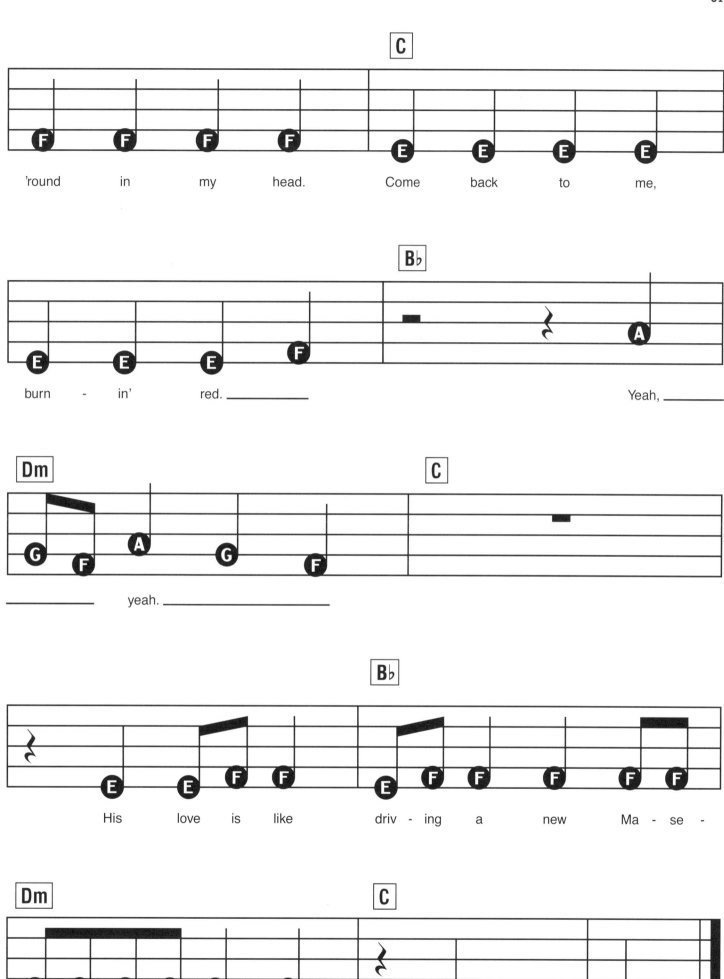

Speak Now

Registration 4
Rhythm: 8-Beat or Rock

Words and Music by
Taylor Swift

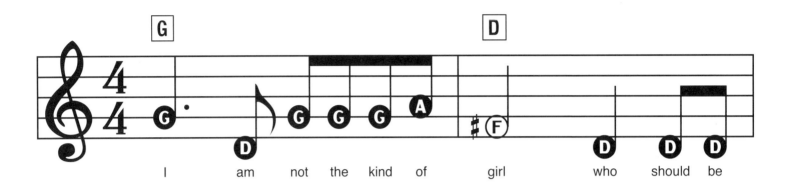

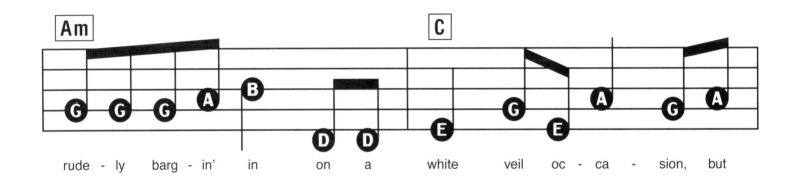

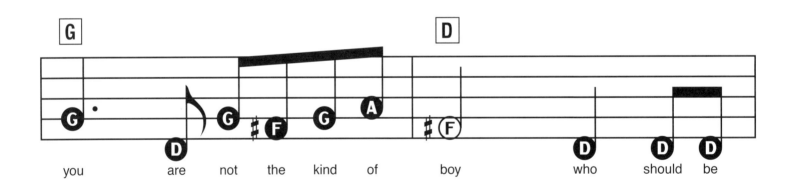

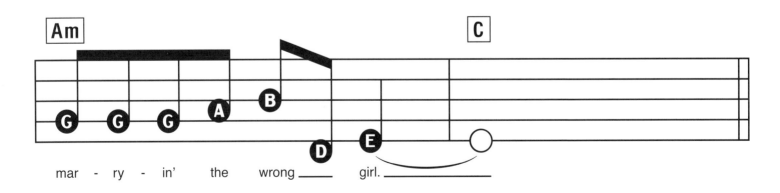

53

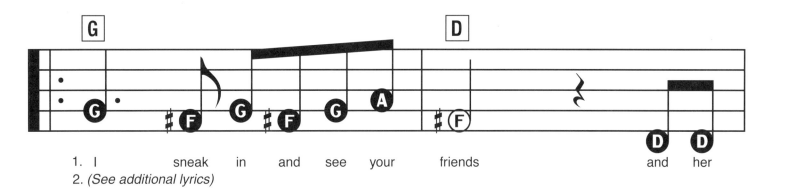

1. I sneak in and see your friends and her
2. *(See additional lyrics)*

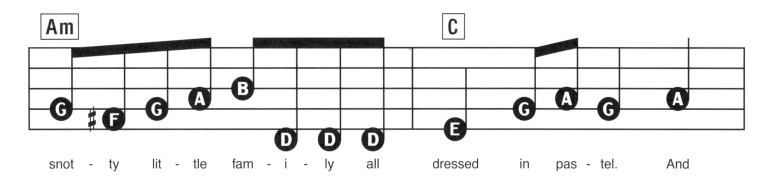

snot - ty lit - tle fam - i - ly all dressed in pas - tel. And

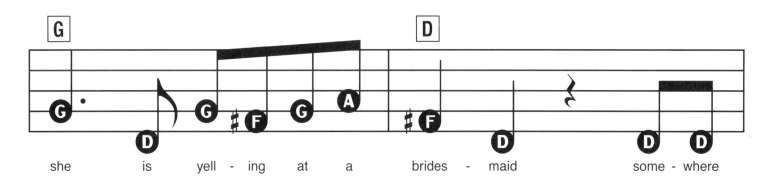

she is yell - ing at a brides - maid some - where

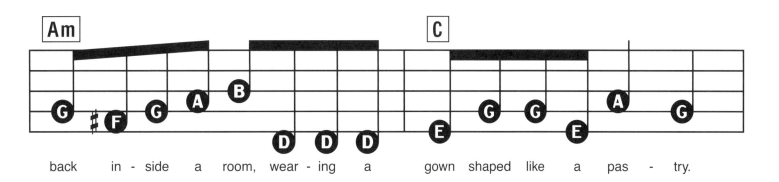

back in - side a room, wear - ing a gown shaped like a pas - try.

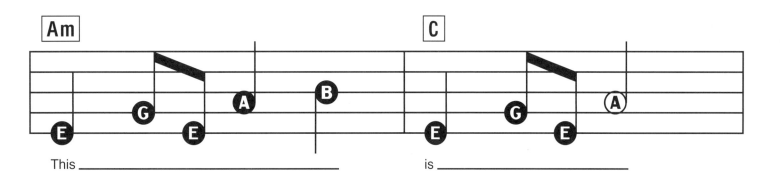

This _____ is _____

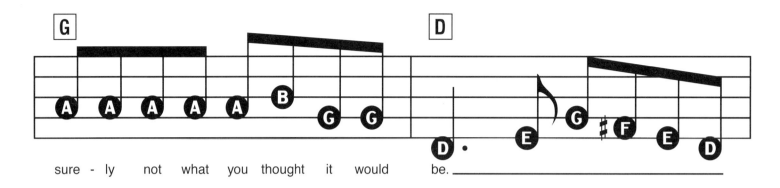

sure - ly not what you thought it would be. _____

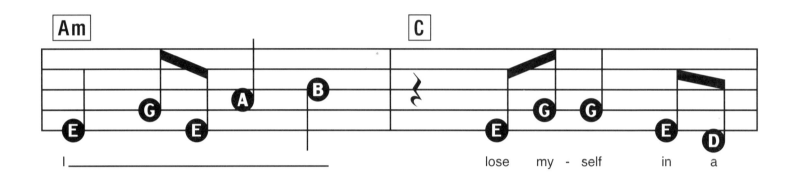

I _____ lose my - self in a

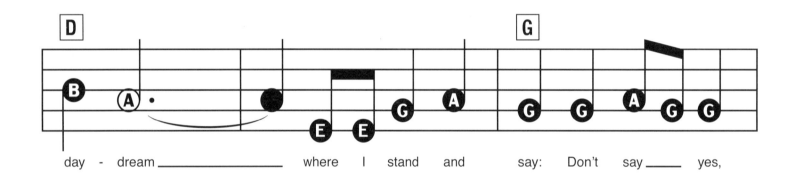

day - dream _____ where I stand and say: Don't say ___ yes,

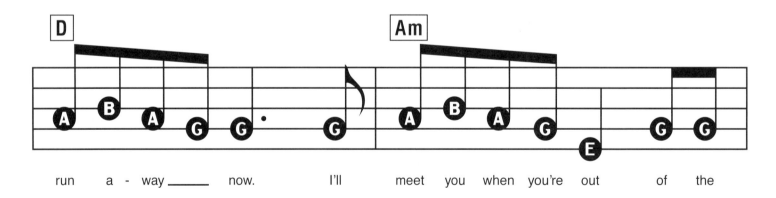

run a - way ___ now. I'll meet you when you're out of the

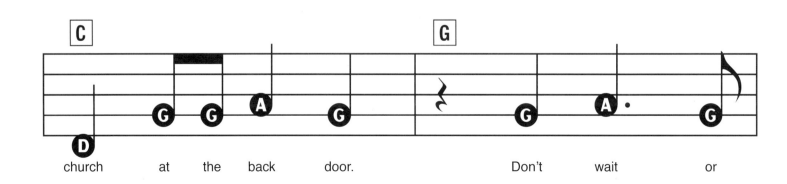

church at the back door. Don't wait or

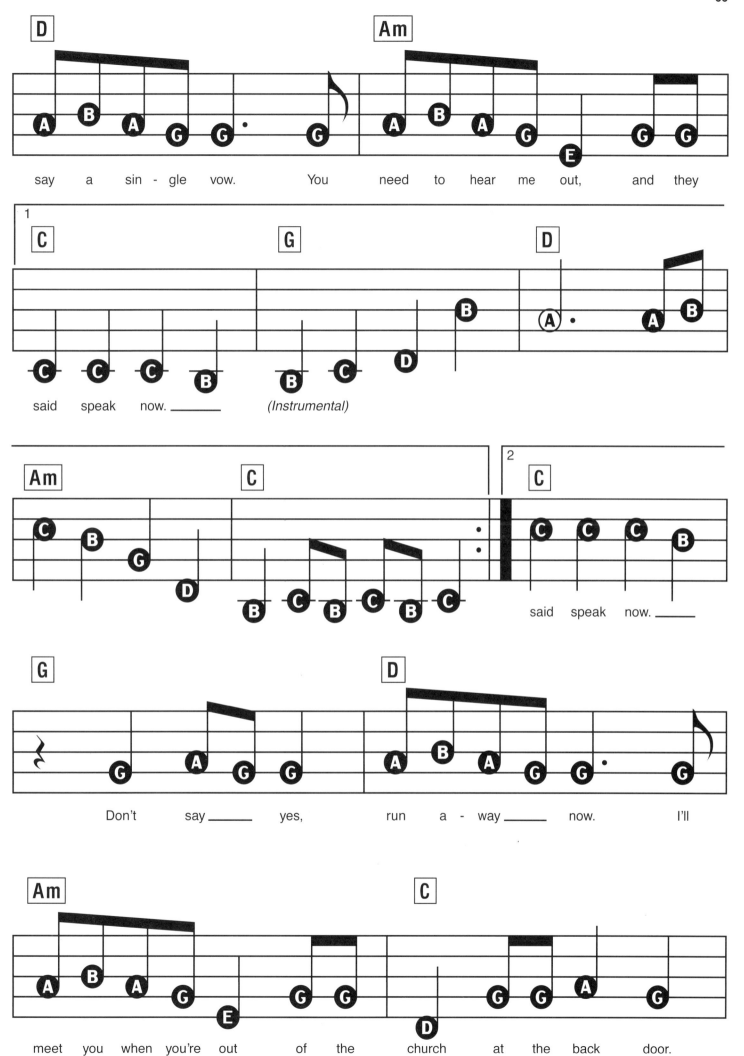

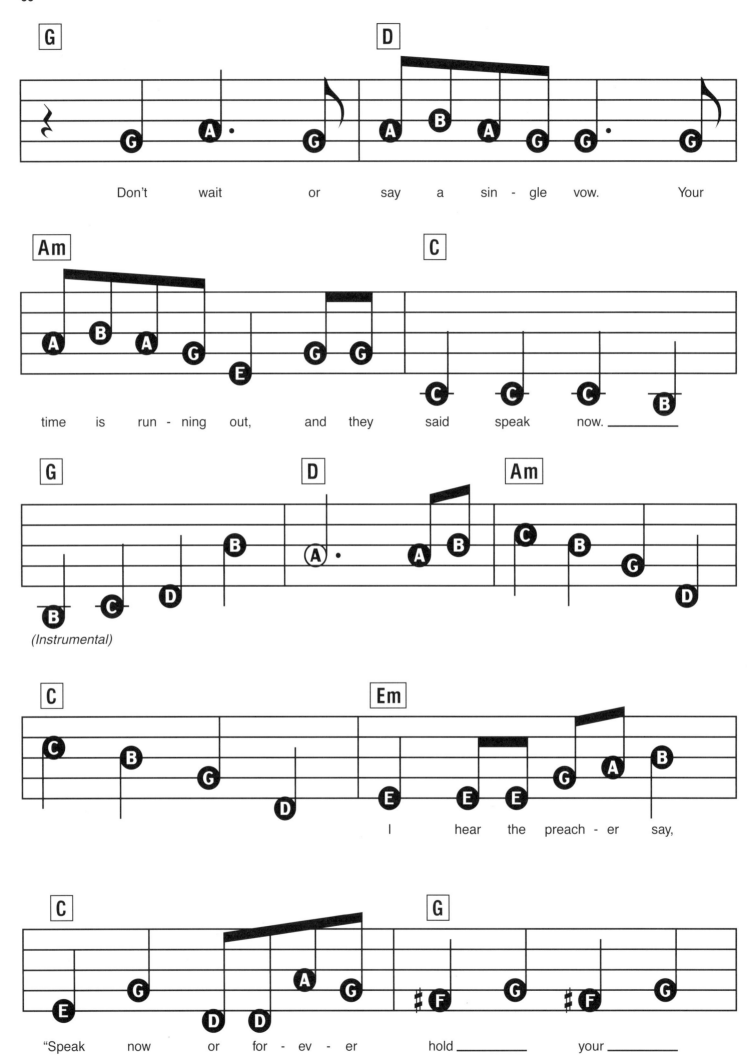

Don't wait or say a sin - gle vow. Your

time is run - ning out, and they said speak now. _____

(Instrumental)

I hear the preach - er say,

"Speak now or for - ev - er hold _____ your _____

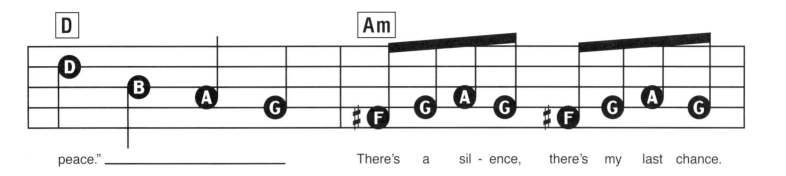

peace." _____ There's a sil - ence, there's my last chance.

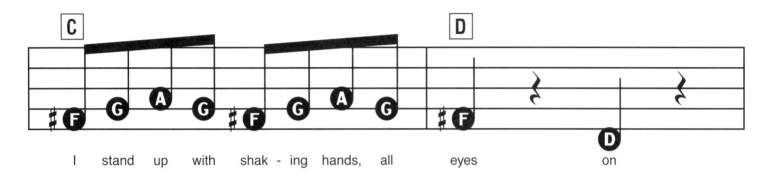

I stand up with shak - ing hands, all eyes on

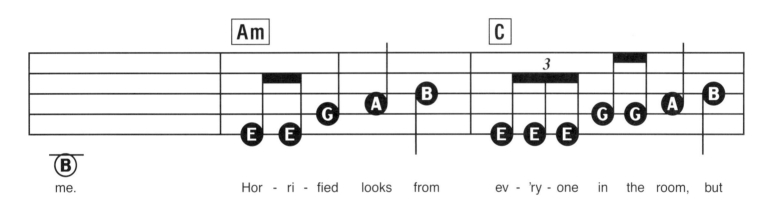

me. Hor - ri - fied looks from ev - 'ry - one in the room, but

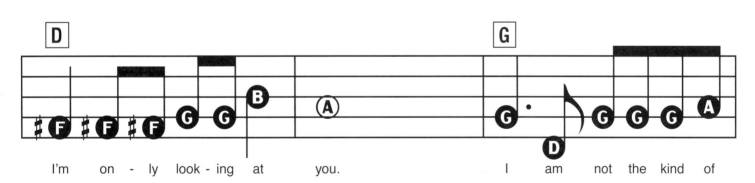

I'm on - ly look - ing at you. I am not the kind of

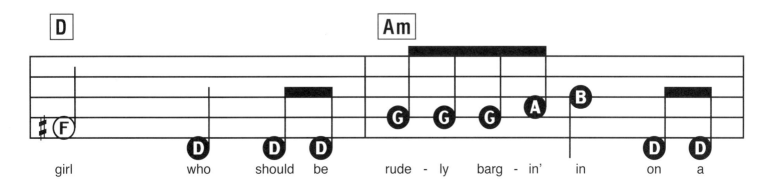

girl who should be rude - ly barg - in' in on a

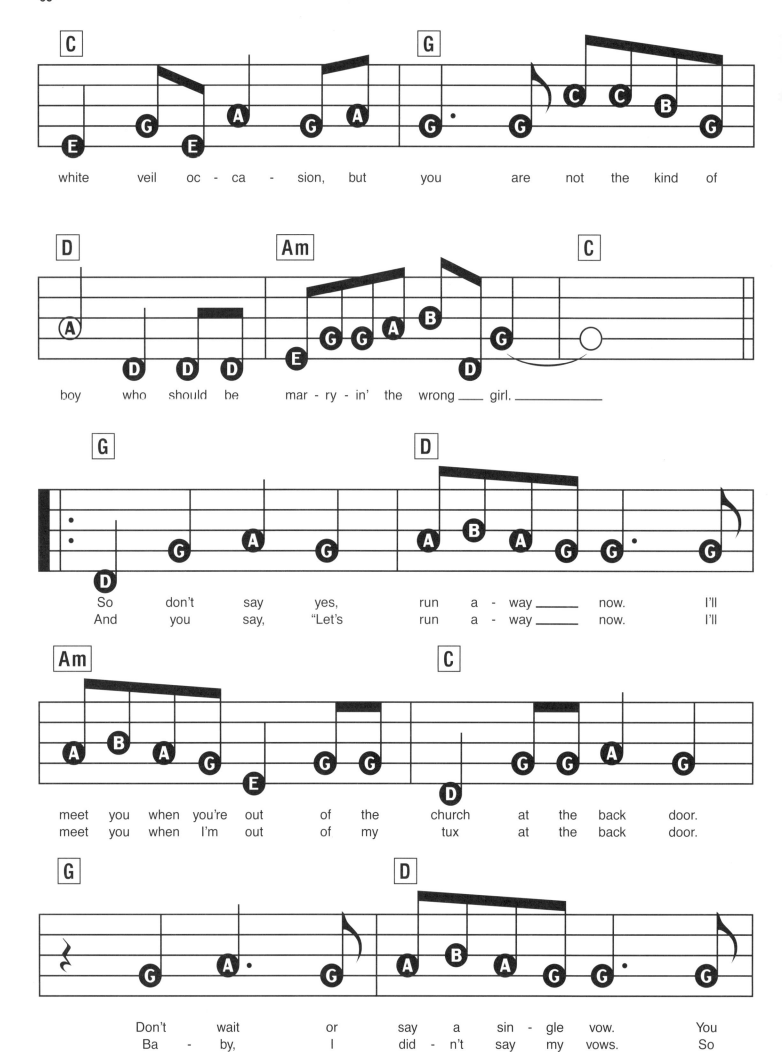

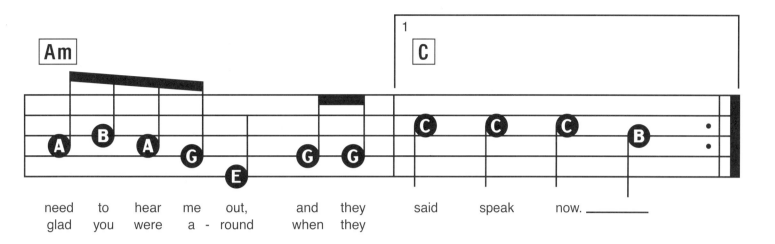

need to hear me out, and they said speak now. _____
glad you were a - round and when they

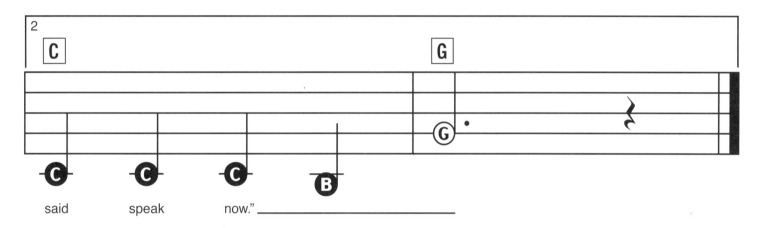

said speak now." _____

Additional Lyrics

2. Fond gestures are exchanged
   And the organ starts to play a song
   That sounds like a death march.
   And I am hiding in the curtains.
   It seems that I was uninvited by your
   Lovely bride-to-be.
   She floats down the aisle
   Like a pageant queen.
   But I know you wish it was me.
   You wish it was me, don't you?

   Don't say yes, run away now…

Starlight

Registration 4
Rhythm: Rock or Dance

Words and Music by
Taylor Swift

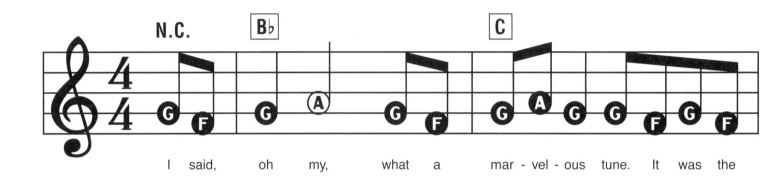

I said, oh my, what a mar - vel - ous tune. It was the

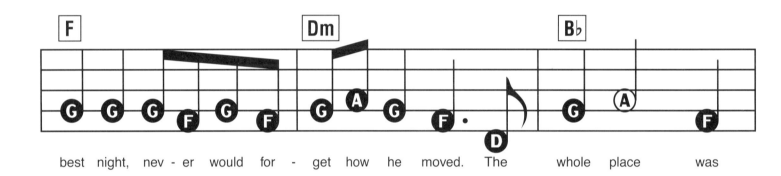

best night, nev - er would for - get how he moved. The whole place was

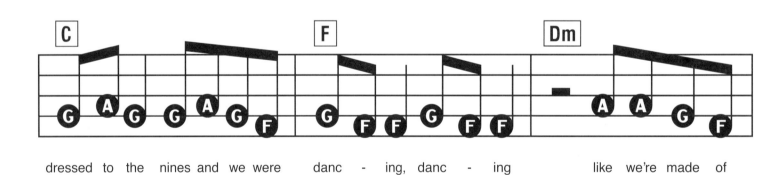

dressed to the nines and we were danc - ing, danc - ing like we're made of

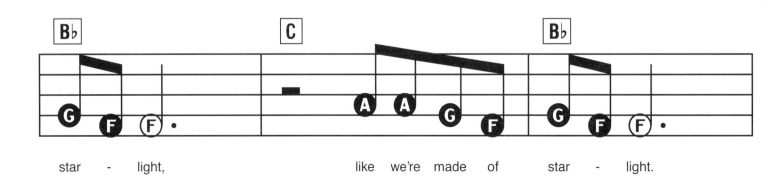

star - light, like we're made of star - light.

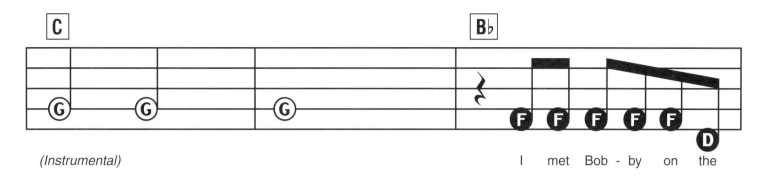

(Instrumental) I met Bob - by on the

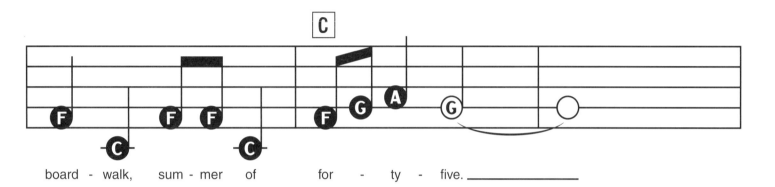

board - walk, sum - mer of for - ty - five. _____

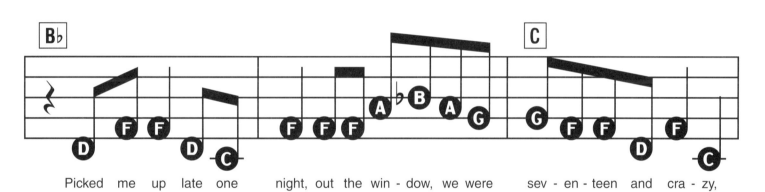

Picked me up late one night, out the win - dow, we were sev - en - teen and cra - zy,

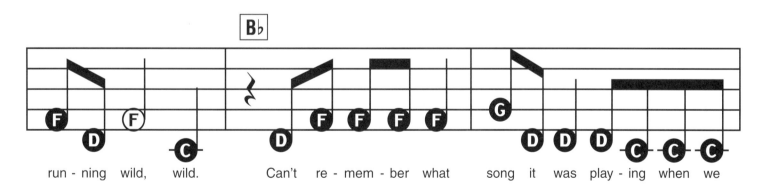

run - ning wild, wild. Can't re - mem - ber what song it was play - ing when we

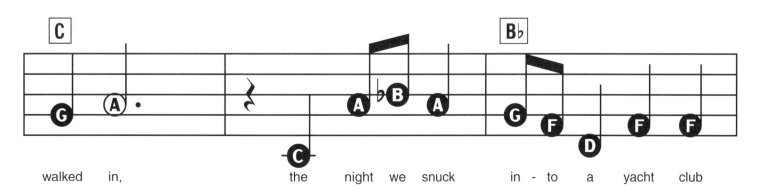

walked in, the night we snuck in - to a yacht club

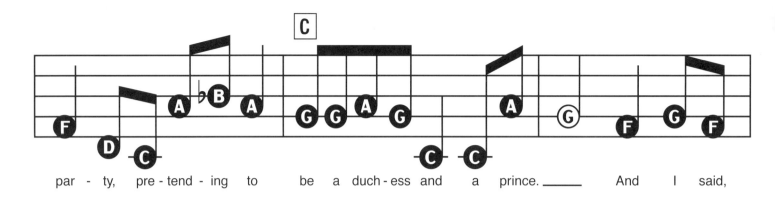

par - ty, pre - tend - ing to be a duch - ess and a prince. _____ And I said,

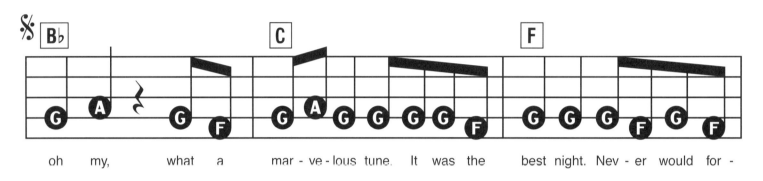

oh my, what a mar - ve - lous tune. It was the best night. Nev - er would for -

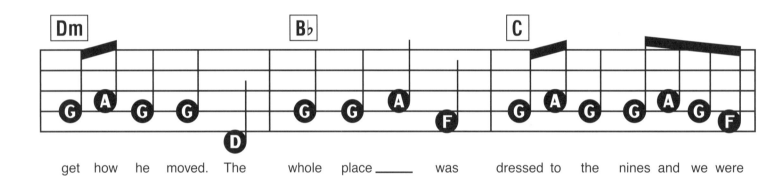

get how he moved. The whole place _____ was dressed to the nines and we were

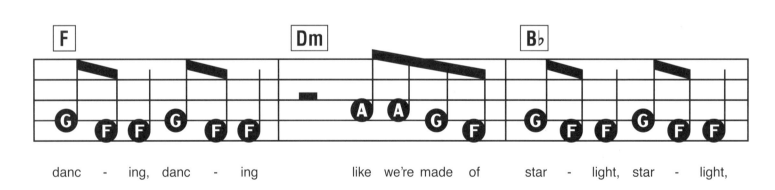

danc - ing, danc - ing like we're made of star - light, star - light,

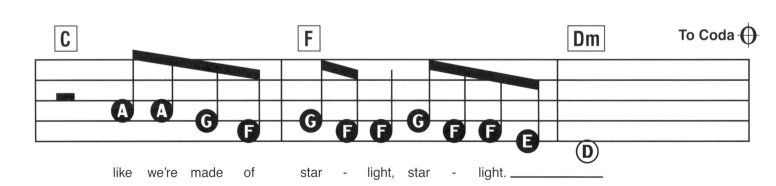

like we're made of star - light, star - light. _____

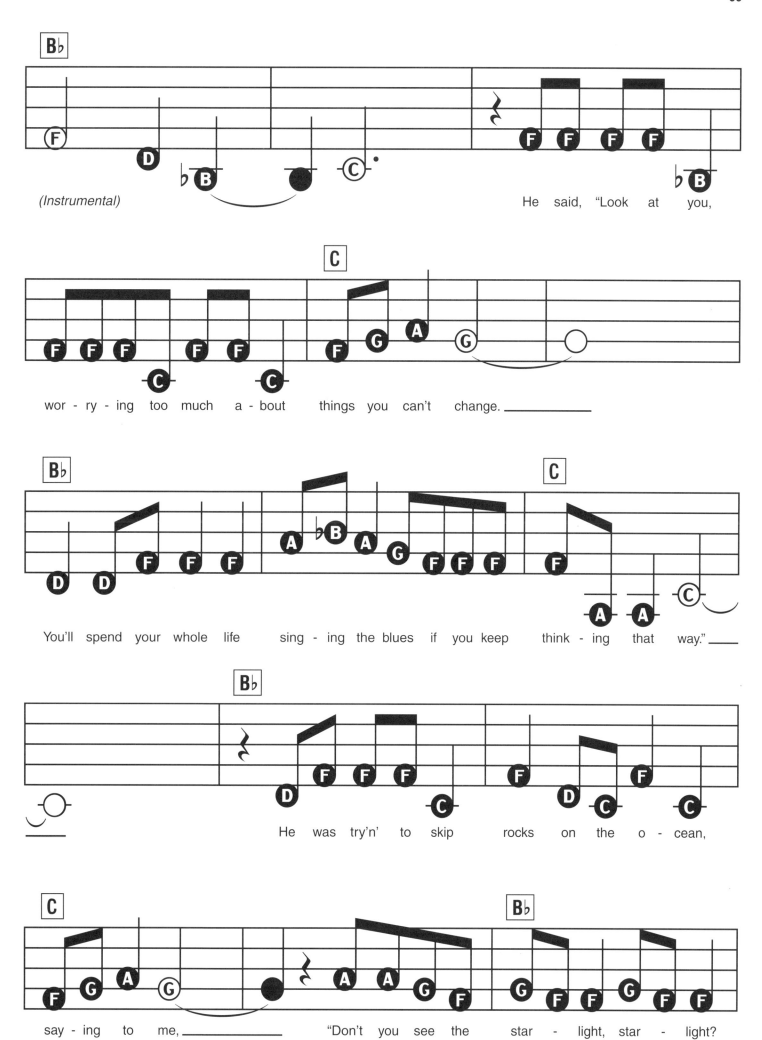

D.S. al Coda
(Return to 𝄋
Play to ⊕ and
Skip to Coda)

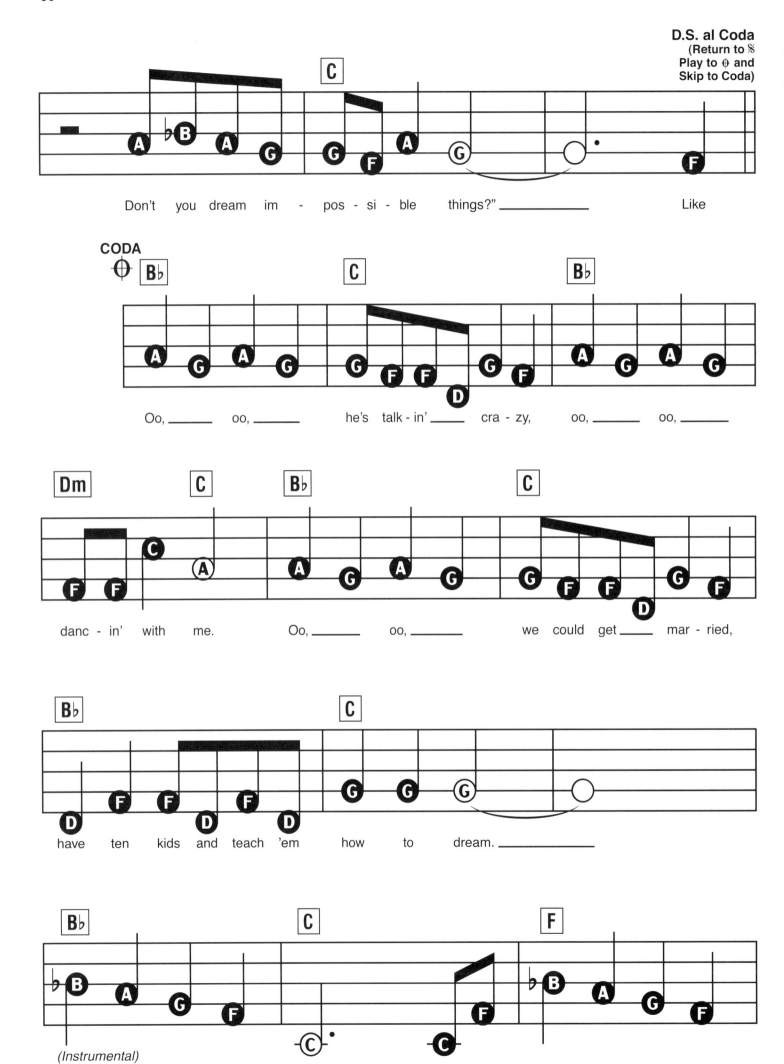

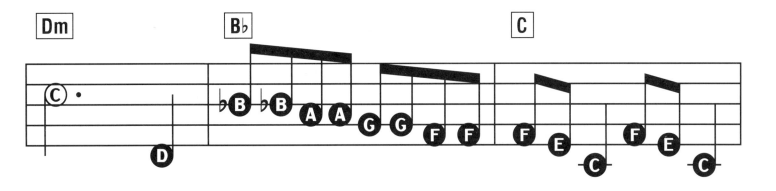

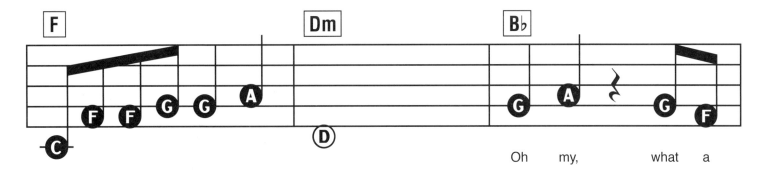

Oh my, what a

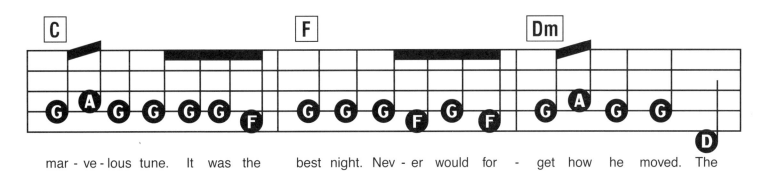

mar - ve - lous tune. It was the best night. Nev - er would for - get how he moved. The

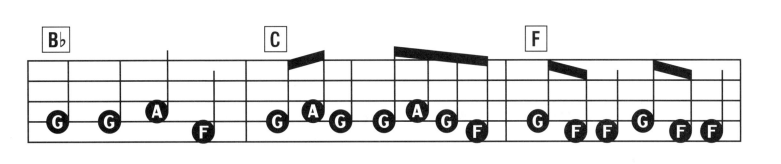

whole place _____ was dressed to the nines and we were danc - ing, danc - ing

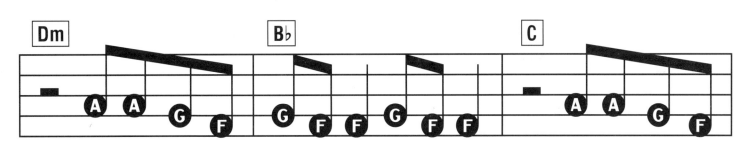

like we're made of star - light, star - light, like we're made of

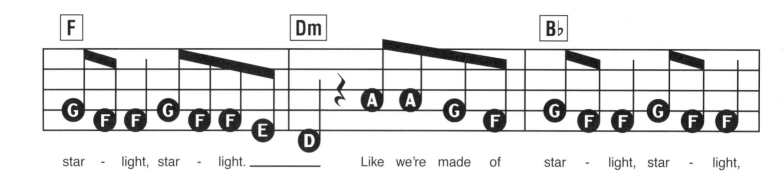

star - light, star - light. _____ Like we're made of star - light, star - light,

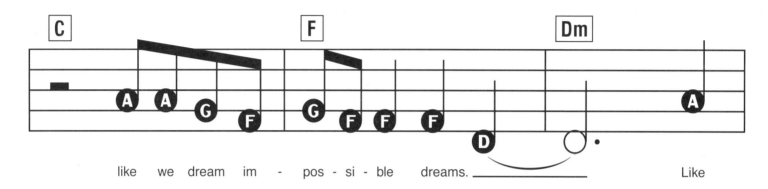

like we dream im - pos - si - ble dreams. _____ Like

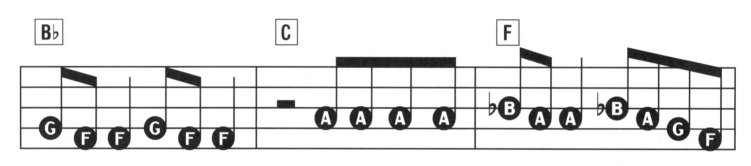

star - light, star - light, like we dream im - pos - si - ble dreams. _____

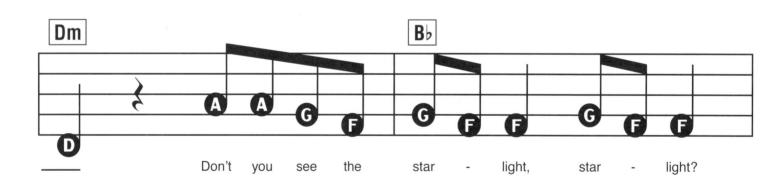

_____ Don't you see the star - light, star - light?

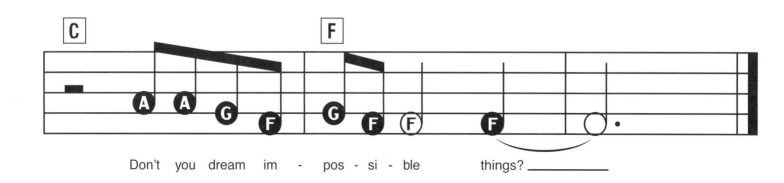

Don't you dream im - pos - si - ble things? _____

Today Was a Fairytale
from VALENTINE'S DAY

Registration 4
Rhythm: 8-Beat or Rock

Words and Music by
Taylor Swift

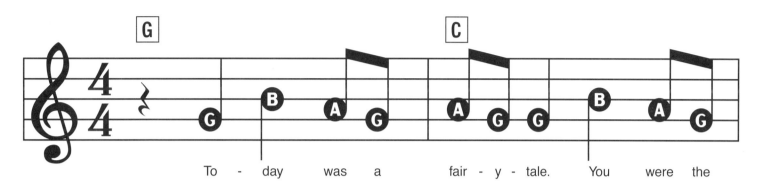

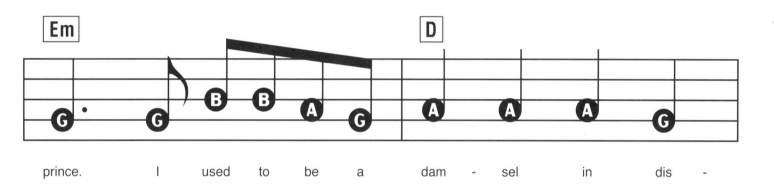

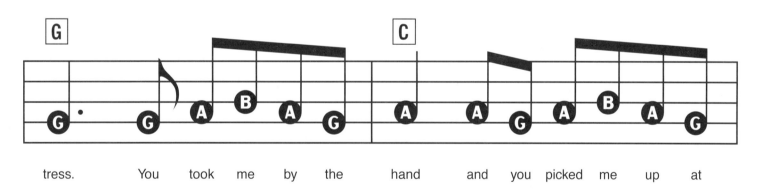

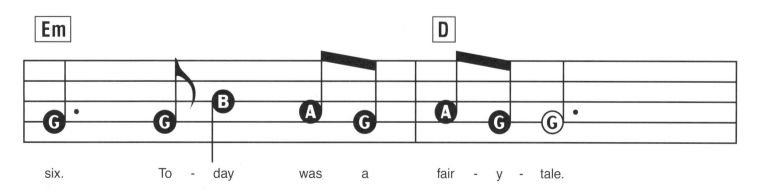

68

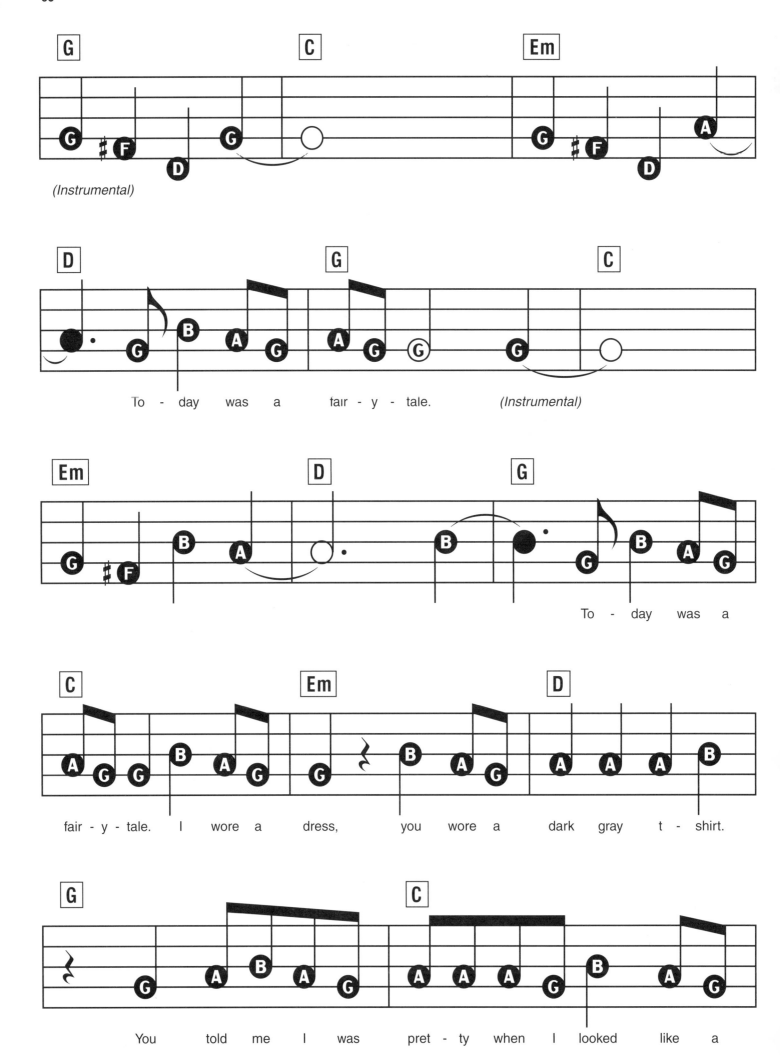

(Instrumental)

To - day was a fair - y - tale. (Instrumental)

To - day was a

fair - y - tale. I wore a dress, you wore a dark gray t - shirt.

You told me I was pret - ty when I looked like a

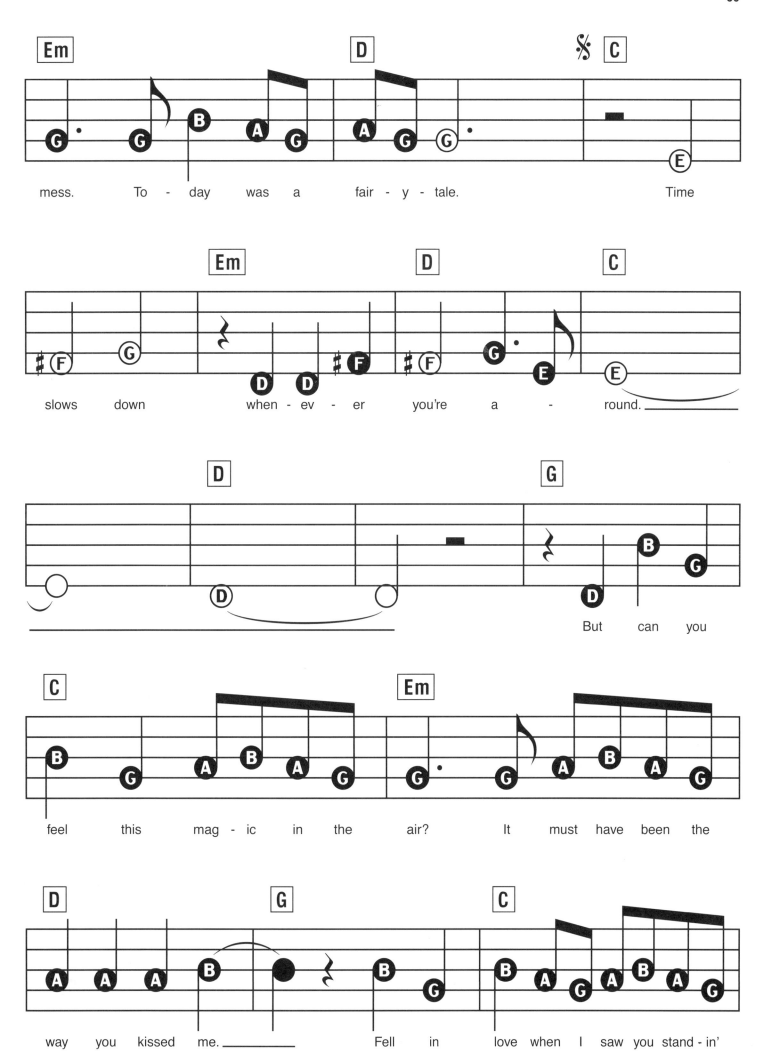

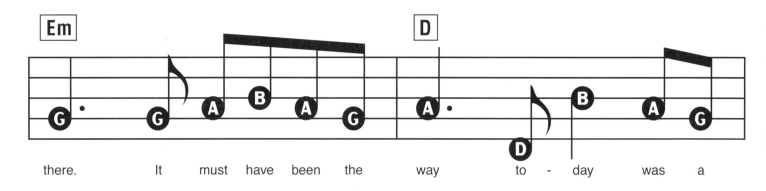

there. It must have been the way to - day was a

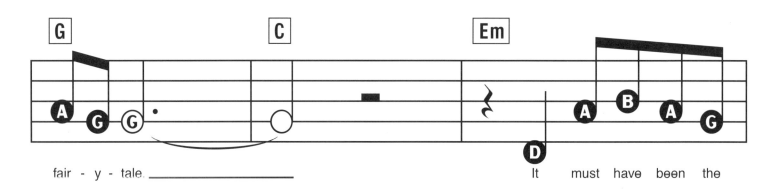

fair - y - tale. _____ It must have been the

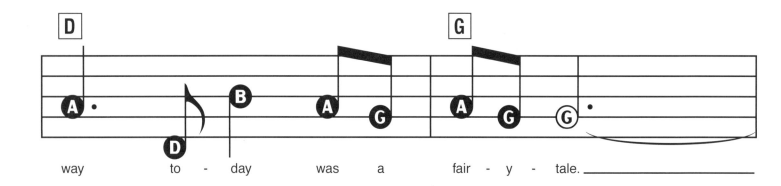

way to - day was a fair - y - tale. _____

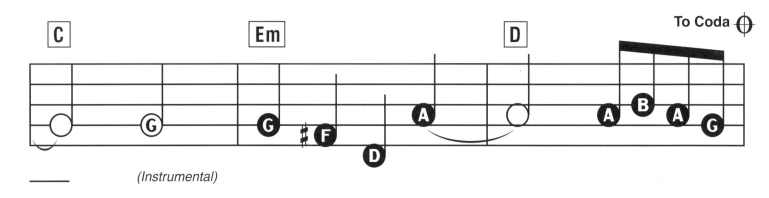

_____ (Instrumental)

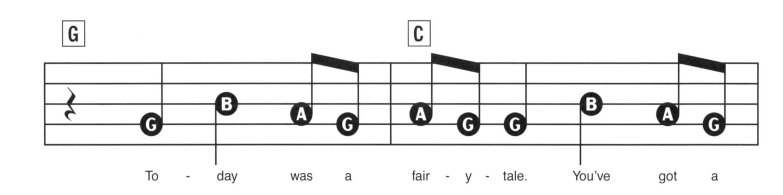

To - day was a fair - y - tale. You've got a

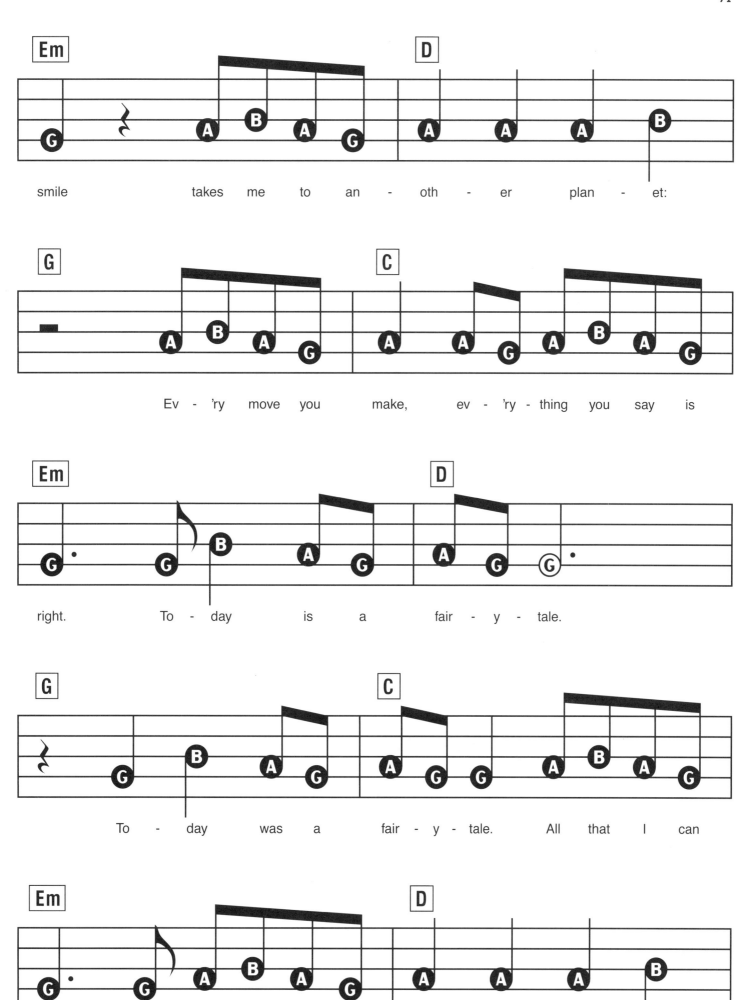

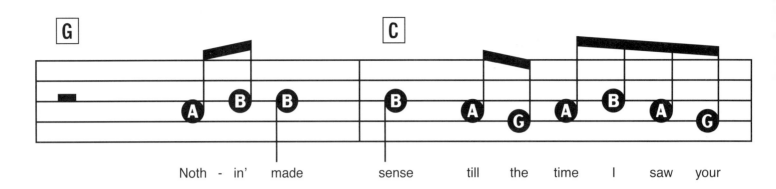

Noth - in' made sense till the time I saw your

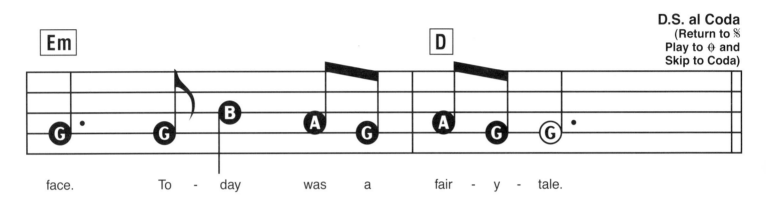

D.S. al Coda
(Return to 𝄋
Play to ⊕ and
Skip to Coda)

face. To - day was a fair - y - tale.

CODA

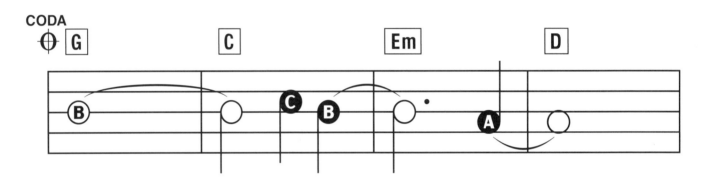

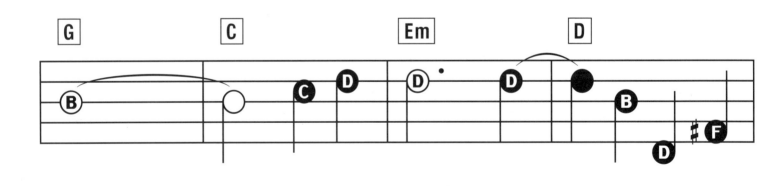

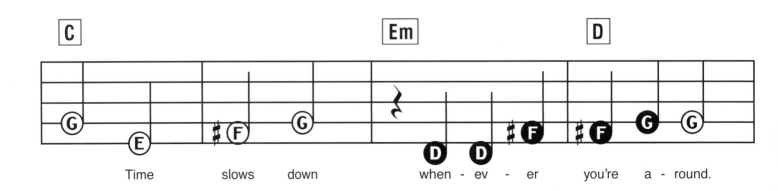

Time slows down when - ev - er you're a - round.

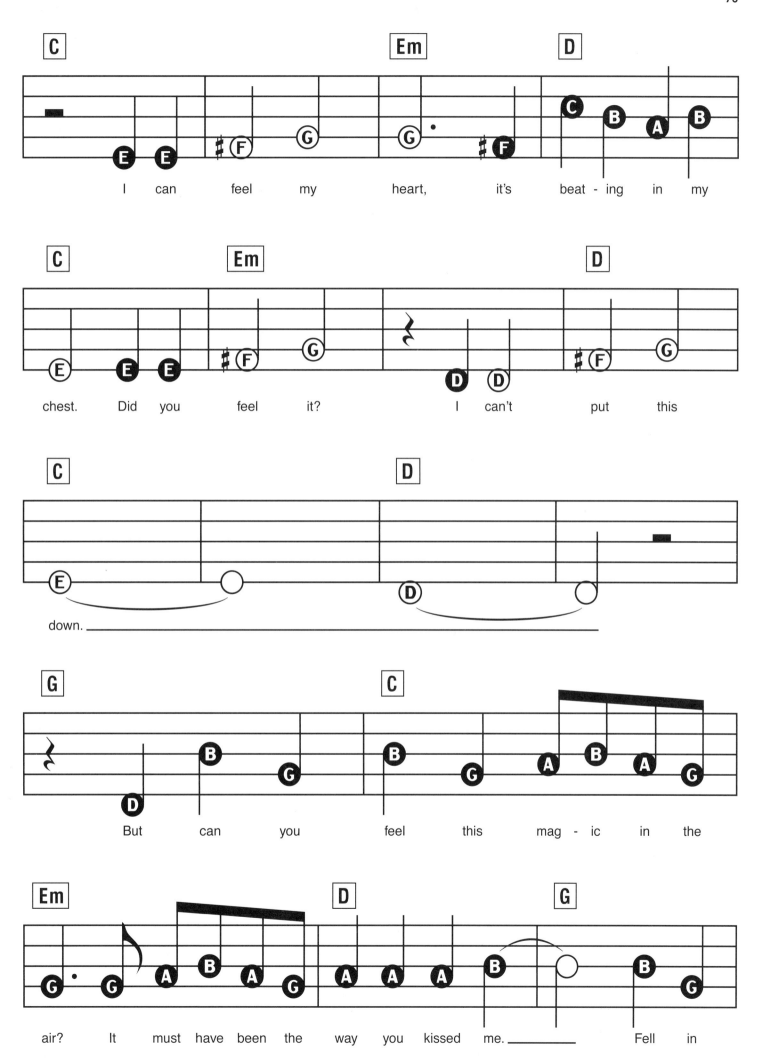

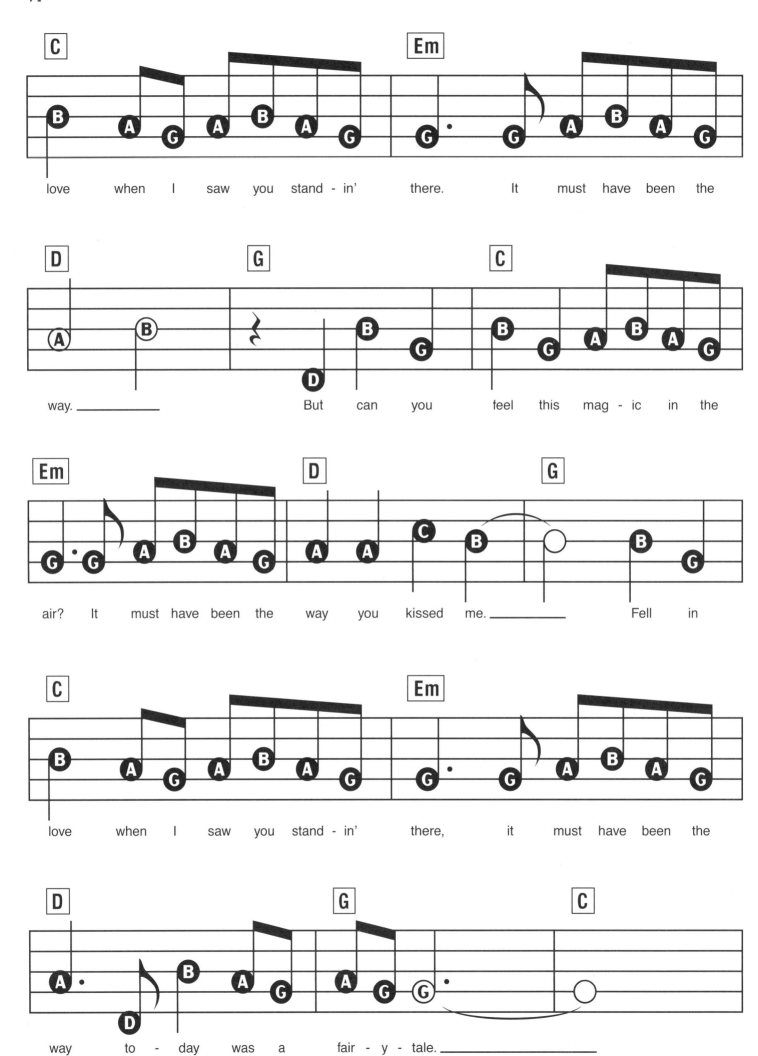

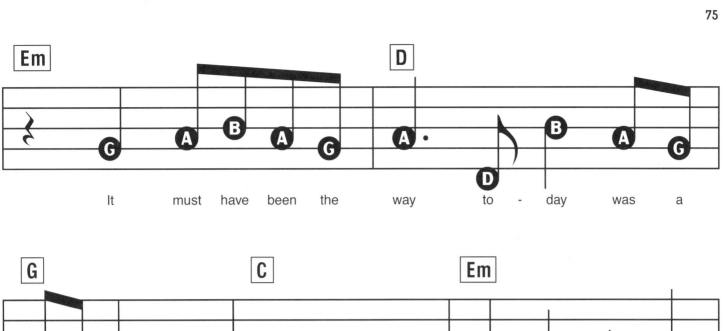

It must have been the way to-day was a

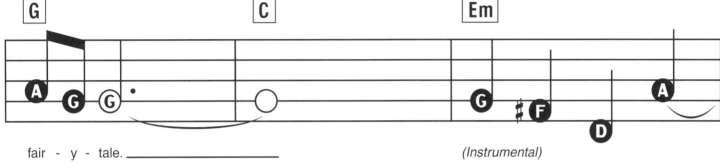

fair - y - tale. _____ (Instrumental)

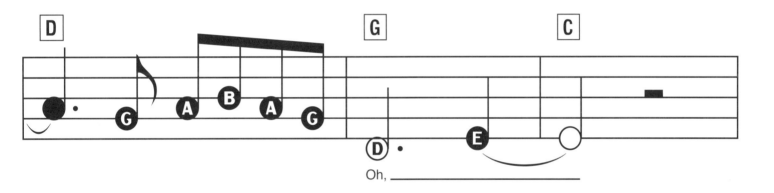

Oh, _____

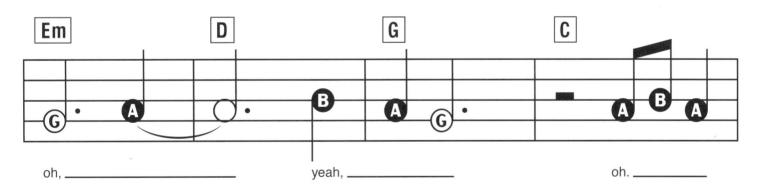

oh, _____ yeah, _____ oh. _____

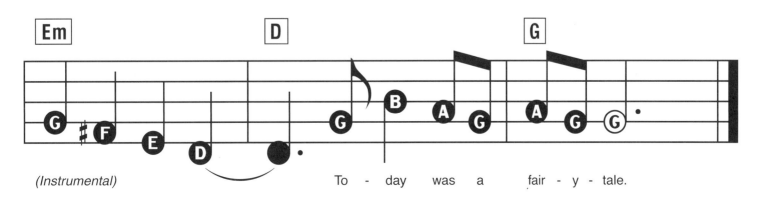

(Instrumental) To - day was a fair - y - tale.

Stay Stay Stay

Registration 4
Rhythm: Rock or 4-Beat

Words and Music by
Taylor Swift

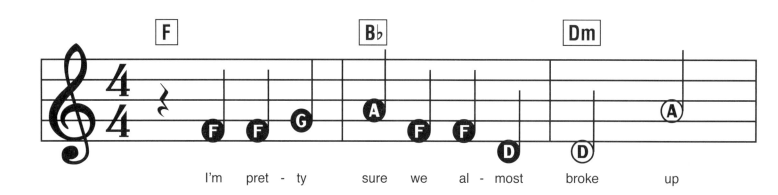

I'm pret - ty   sure   we   al - most   broke   up

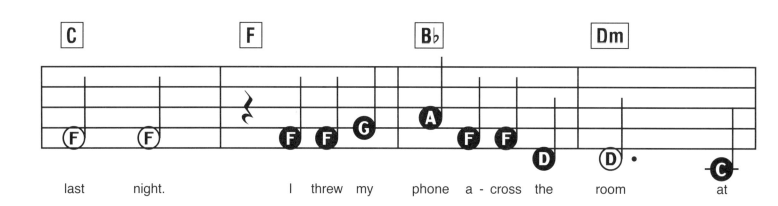

last   night.   I   threw   my   phone   a - cross   the   room   at

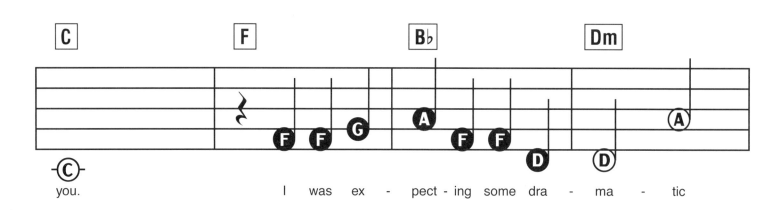

you.   I   was   ex - pect - ing   some   dra - ma - tic

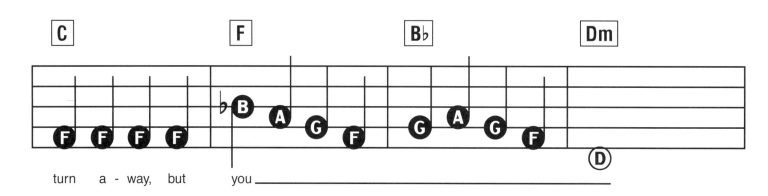

turn   a - way,   but   you _____

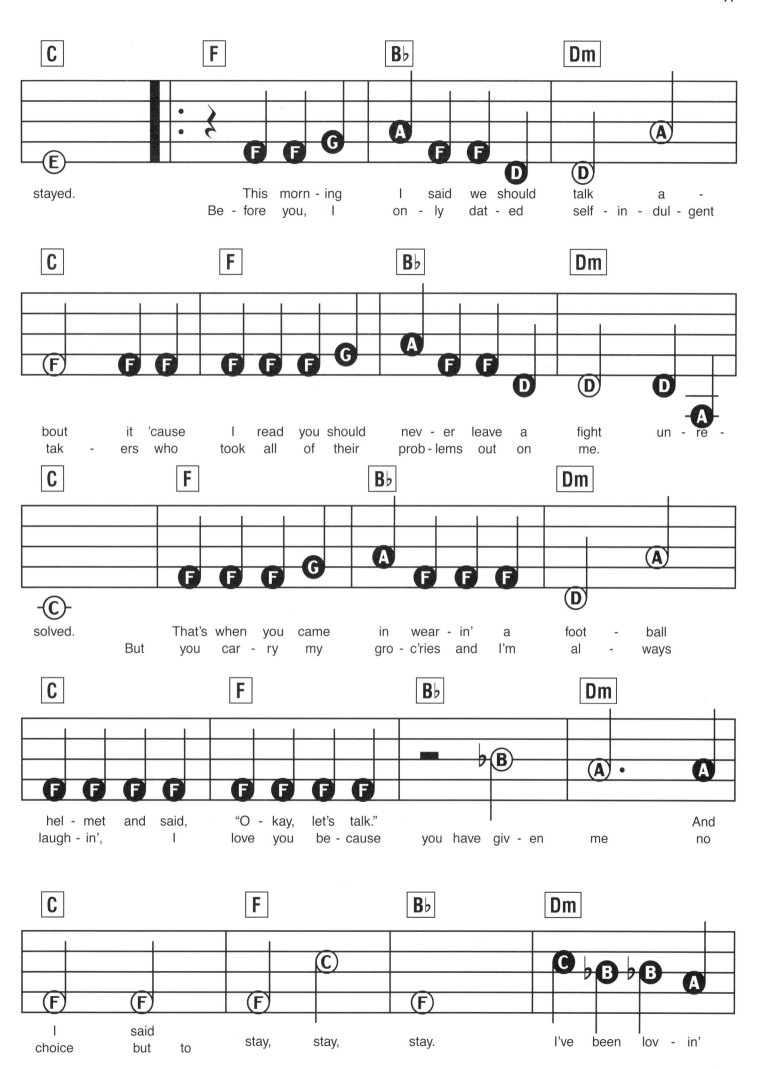

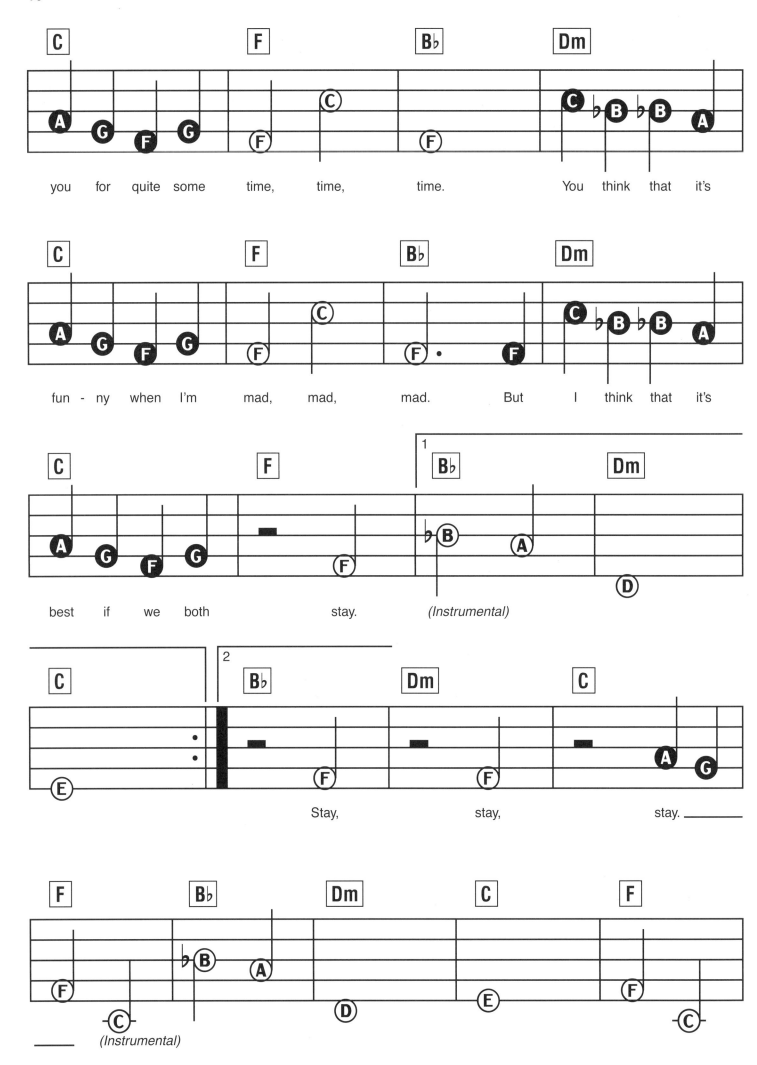

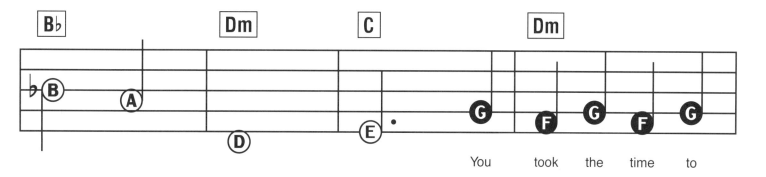

C F B♭ Dm
you for quite some time, time, time. You think that it's
C F B♭ Dm
fun - ny when I'm mad, mad, mad. But I think that it's
C F 1 B♭ Dm
best if we both stay. (Instrumental)
C 2 B♭ Dm C
Stay, stay, stay.
F B♭ Dm C F
(Instrumental)

You took the time to

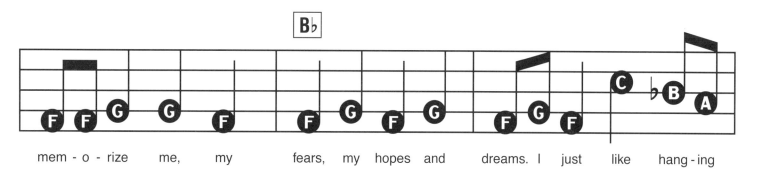

mem - o - rize me, my fears, my hopes and dreams. I just like hang - ing

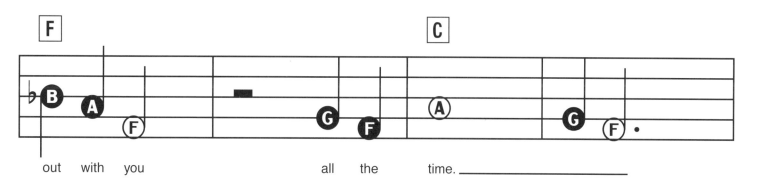

out with you all the time. _____

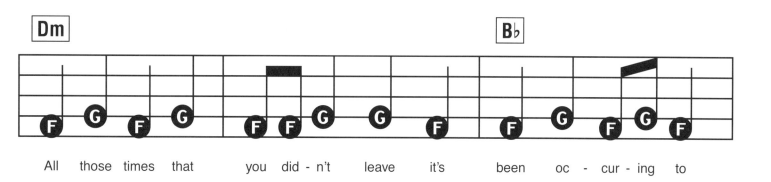

All those times that you did - n't leave it's been oc - cur - ing to

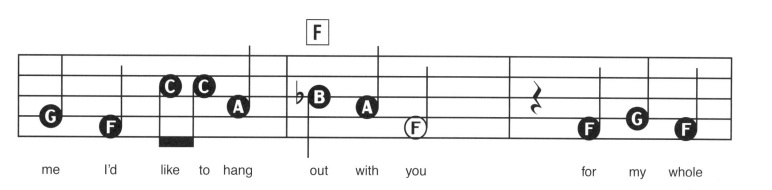

me I'd like to hang out with you for my whole

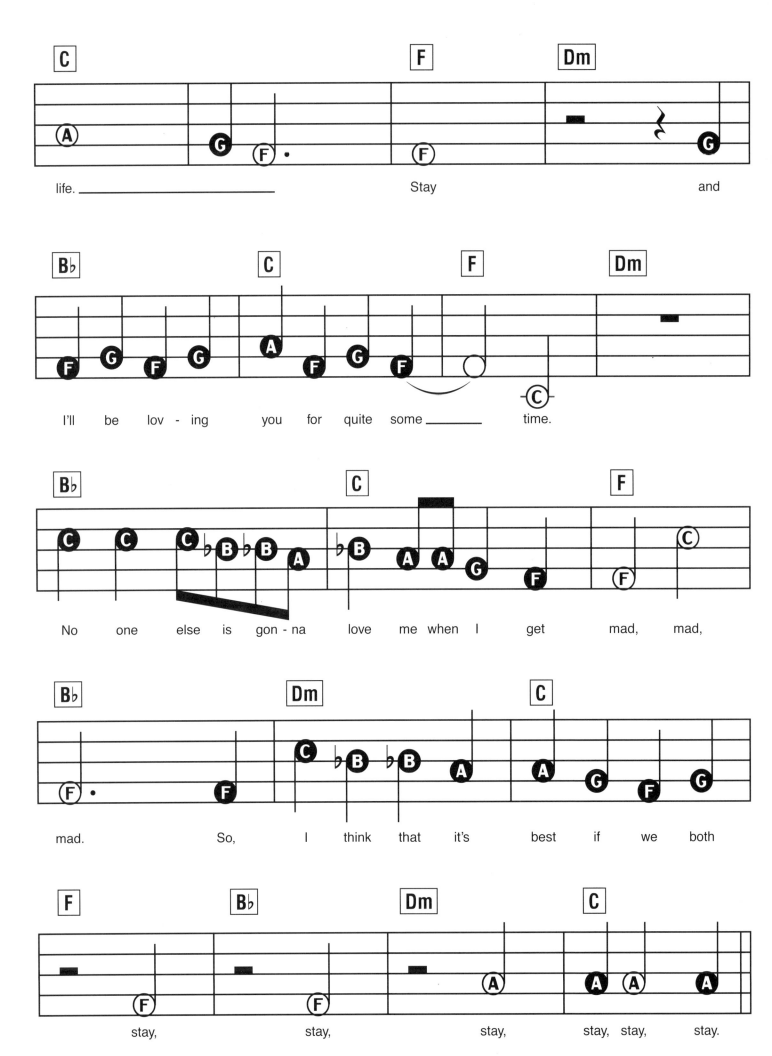

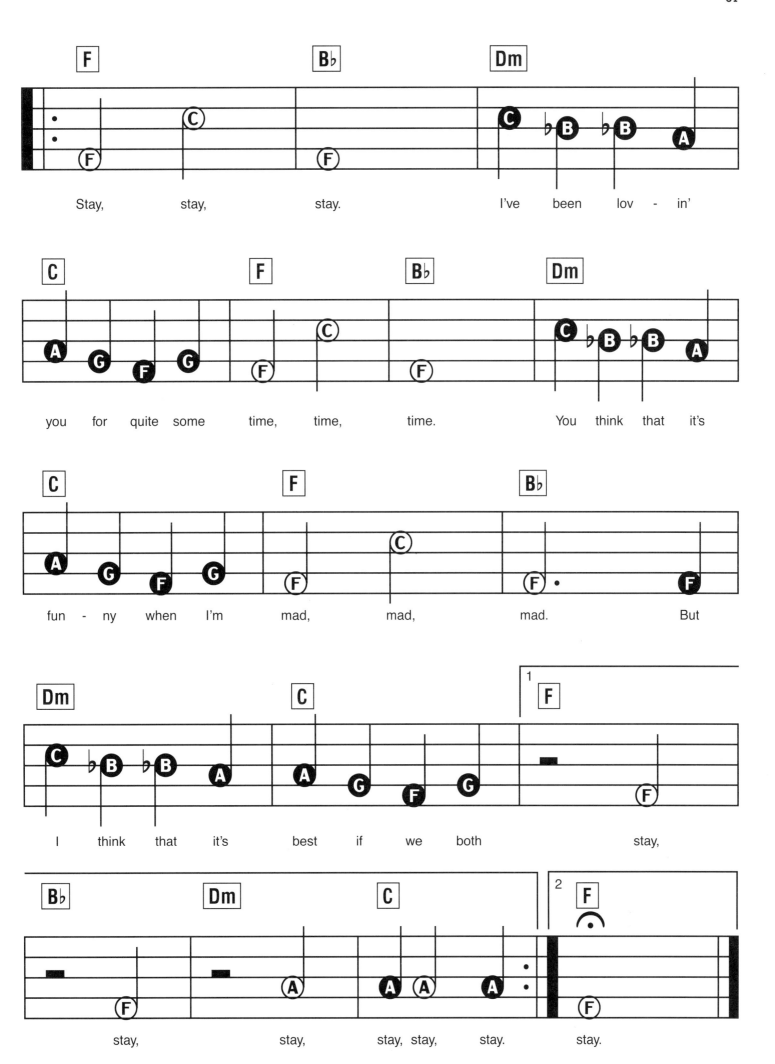

We Are Never Ever Getting Back Together

Registration 4
Rhythm: Rock or Dance

Words and Music by Taylor Swift,
Shellback and Max Martin

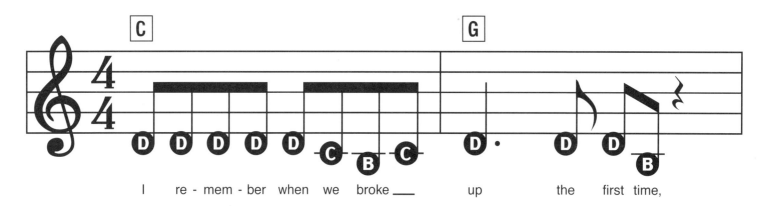

I re-mem-ber when we broke ___ up the first time,

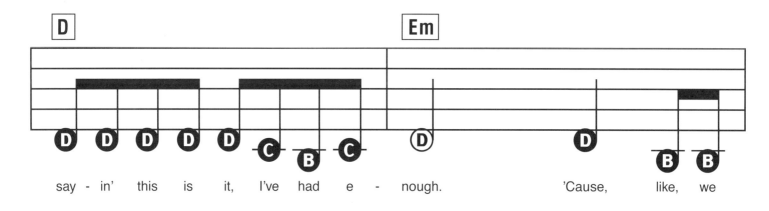

say - in' this is it, I've had e - nough. 'Cause, like, we

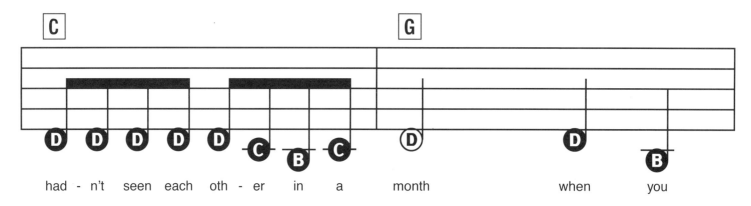

had - n't seen each oth - er in a month when you

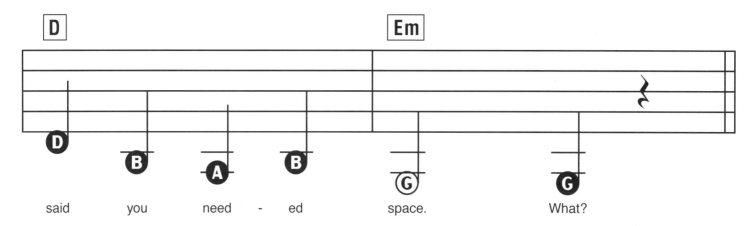

said you need - ed space. What?

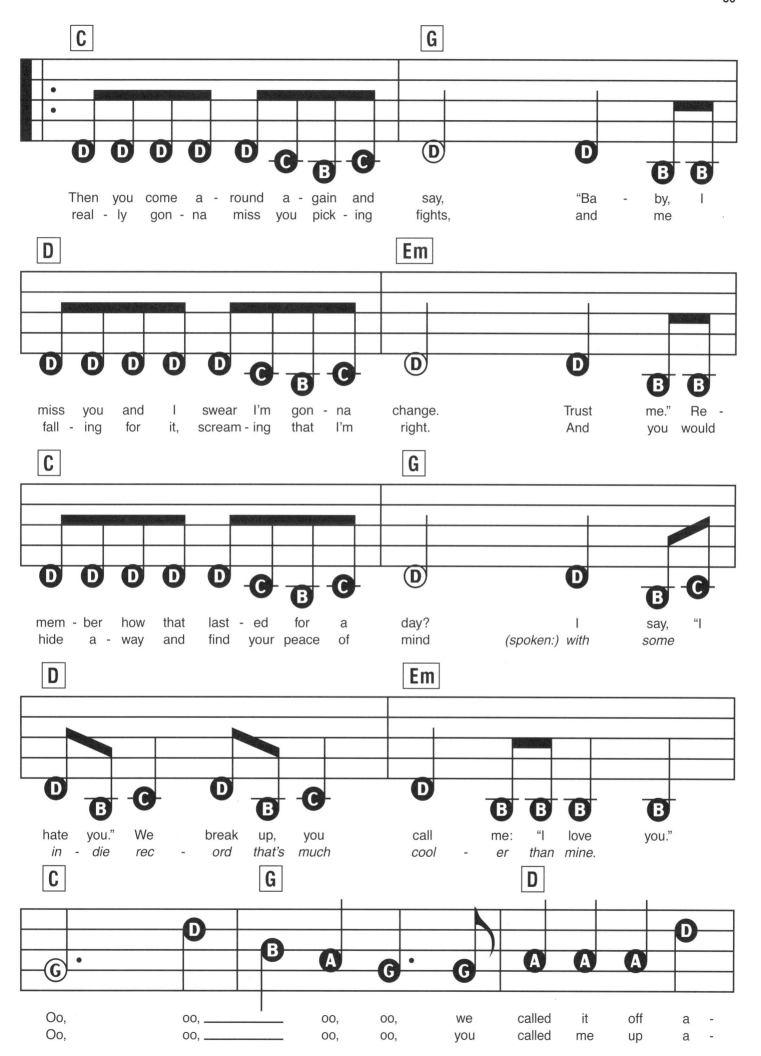

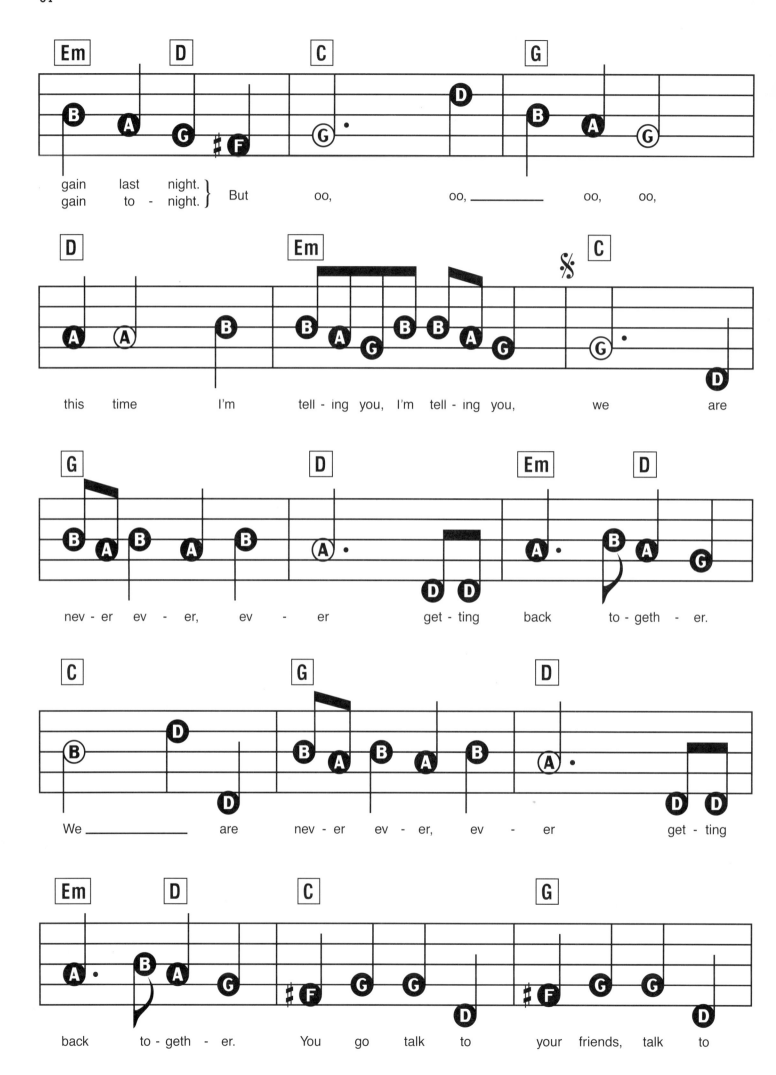

85

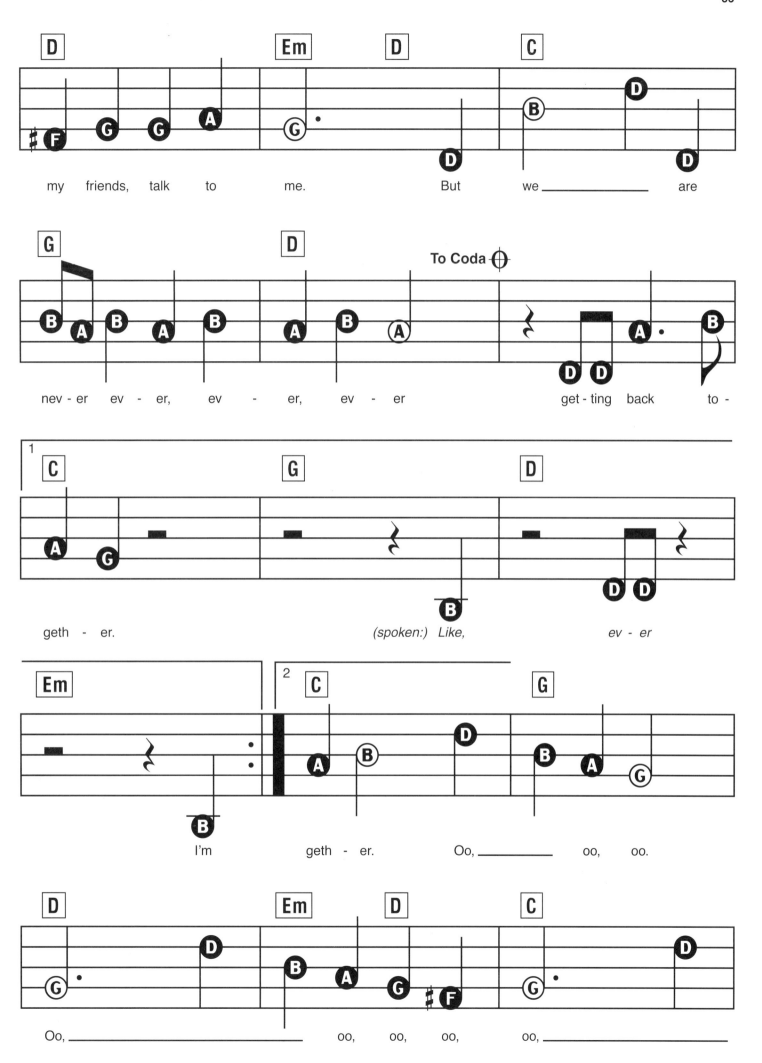

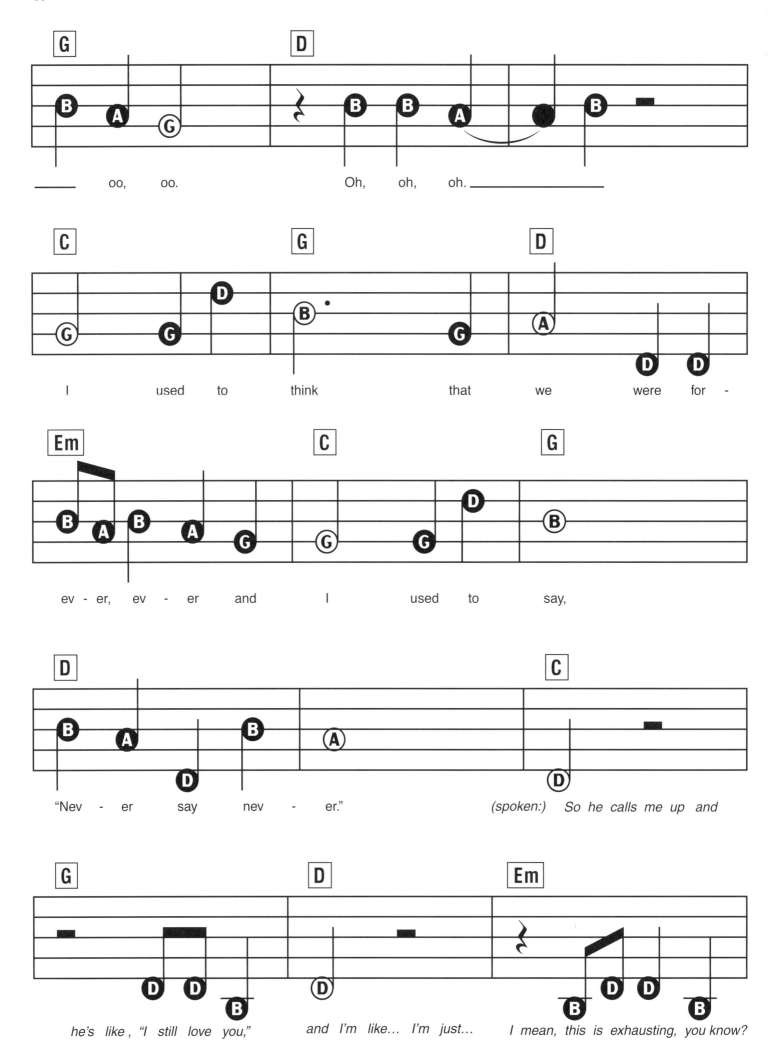

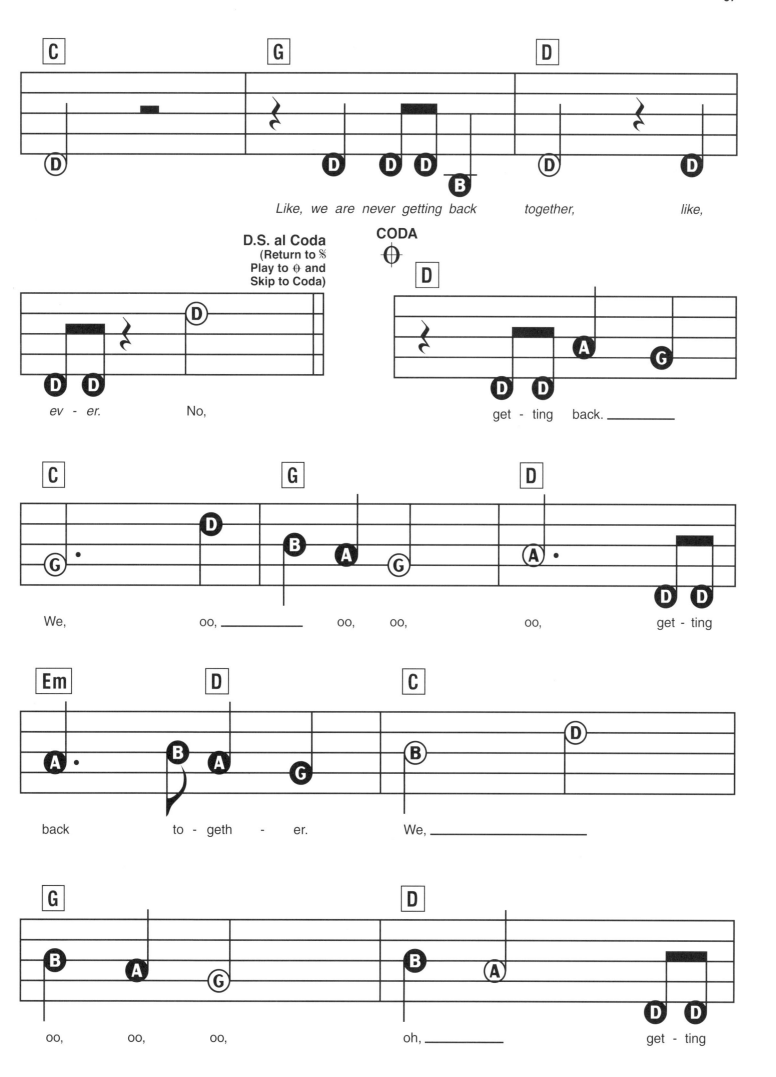

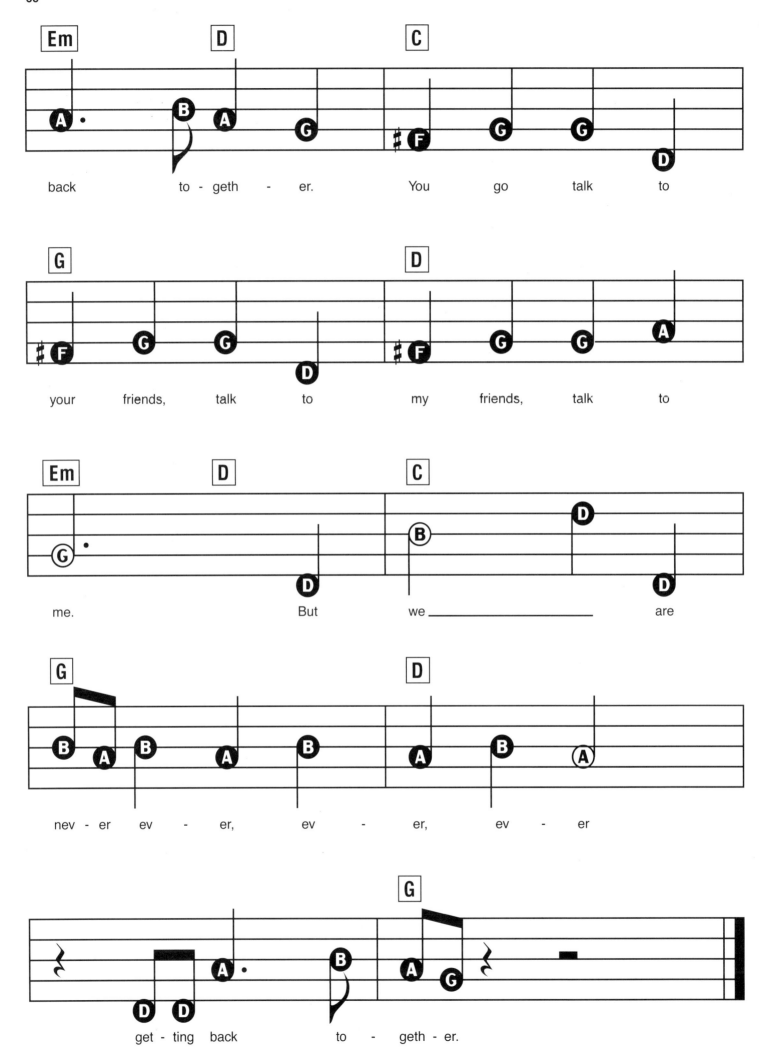